Final Destinations

A Travel Guide for Remarkable Cemeteries
in Texas, New Mexico, Oklahoma,
Arkansas, and Louisiana

Bryan Woolley
Larry Bleiberg
Leon Unruh
Jean Simmons
Tom Simmons
Kathryn Straach
Bob Bersano

University of North Texas Press
Denton, Texas

Printed by permission of *The Dallas Morning News* from
The Dallas Morning News Travel Section

Printed in the United States of America

5 4 3 2 1

Requests for permission to reproduce material from this work should be sent to:

Permissions
University of North Texas Press
PO Box 311336
Denton TX 76203-1336
940-565-2142

The paper in this book meets the minimum requirements of the American National
Standard for Permanence of Paper for Printed Library Materials, Z39.48.1984

Library of Congress Cataloging-in-Publication Data

Final destinations : a travel guide for remarkable cemeteries in Texas, New Mexico,
Oklahoma, Arkansas, and Louisiana / written by Bryan Woolley . . . [et al.].
p. cm.
Includes index.
ISBN 1-57441-085-7 (alk. Paper)
1. Cemeteries—Texas—Guidebooks. 2. Cemeteries—New Mexico—Guidebooks.
3. Cemeteries—Oklahoma—Guidebooks. 4. Cemeteries—Arkansas—Guidebooks.
5. Cemeteries—Louisiana—Guidebooks. 6. Texas—Guidebooks. 7. New Mexico—
Guidebooks. 8. Oklahoma—Guidebooks. 9. Arkansas—Guidebooks.
10. Louisiana—Guidebooks. I. Woolley, Bryan.
F387 .F562000
917.604'43—dc21   99-054198

Unless otherwise noted, all photographs
are used courtesy of *The Dallas Morning News.*
Design by Angela Schmitt

To Karen Jordan
An editor who always goes the extra mile—
and knows a good story when she sees it.

L

Contents

NEW MEXICO

OKLAHOMA

ARKANSAS

LOUISIANA

MORE ON CEMETERIES

Final Destinations

Bryan Woolley

"The people of long ago are not remembered," wrote that hard-eyed realist of 3,000 years ago, the Preacher of Ecclesiastes, "nor will there be any remembrance of people yet to come by those who come after them."

He was right. Neither he nor his name is remembered. Yet we try to remember. We keep old albums, scrapbooks and mementos of those who have died and pass them on to our own heirs. We do genealogical searches. We visit ancestral hometowns. We try to retrace the footsteps of family members who have gone before.

And we visit cemeteries. The Texas Historical Commission estimates there are more than 46,000 cemeteries in Texas alone. And no one knows how many others have been lost. Time, weather and vandals destroy their markers. Forgotten graves get bulldozed and paved over during construction of highways and subdivisions. Neglect allows weeds and brush to reclaim land in which the bones of our ancestors lie.

The cemeteries that remain tell a lot about the people who are buried in them, much more than their names and dates. Many rich people, for example, are as ostentatious in death as they were in life. Their remains lie in granite or marble tombs festooned with ornamentation or guarded by statues of weeping angels mourning the worthy's departure. Many of the rich seem to be trying to assert their superiority over the surrounding dead as they did over their fellow citizens in life. And the graves of the very poor bring a lump to the throat or a tear to the eye of even a stranger. We see crude crosses made of fence pickets or pieces of aluminum molding bought at Kmart, names and dates scratched into wet cement with a nail and the many infant graves in their little cemeteries, dug by neighbors or relatives.

Some cemeteries are lush parks, full of grass and trees and fountains that invite the visitor to pray or meditate or remember. Others are barren and desolate, stark reminders of our mortality. Some, because of individuals buried in them—their fame, their stories, their eccentricities—are historic sites or tourist attractions.

Cemeteries also teach us of the religious beliefs—or lack thereof—of the people in them, and the traditions of their races and cultures, and the meaning of life and death in the wisdom of their communities.

Every cemetery is worth visiting, and the people in them are worth trying to remember. They were much like us.

∞

This book will take you on a tour of some of the best-known and the more obscure cemeteries and gravesites in Texas and its surrounding four states: New Mexico, Oklahoma, Arkansas, and Louisiana. Beginning in lush East Texas, we'll visit the favorite cemetery of the readers of *The Dallas Morning News* Travel section in Scottsville, and many others. Then we move down to the coast to the many fascinating cemeteries in Houston-Galveston and then across to the Dallas-Fort Worth Metroplex, to the resting places of the servants of Texas in Austin, and finally out to the wild west of Texas, where larger-than-life gunmen were really buried with their boots on. Jumping the border into New Mexico, we visit some animal graves, the shrine to D. H. Lawrence in Taos, and some other sites before exploring the grasslands of Oklahoma and its memorials to Will Rogers and Geronimo. Arkansas holds some of the most beautiful cemetery sculpture in the region, as well as several enormous military cemeteries. Finally we come to rest in Louisiana. New Orleans is famous for its above-ground cemeteries, but the bayous of the state also hold mortuary treasures. And to bring us full circle, we end at the graves of two great blues musicians, Leadbelly in Mooringsport, Louisiana, and Blind Lemon Jefferson in Wortham, Texas.

Blind Lemon once sang, "See that my grave is kept clean." This book is a small attempt to help the weekend historian and family genealogist do that. Or at least know that there is a grave and where it lies.

Digging Graves Teaches Basic Cemetery Etiquette

Leon Unruh

My dad taught me how to dig a grave and how to behave around them. As the sexton for our township cemetery in western Kansas, Elgie Unruh opened well over a hundred holes in twenty years.

"There was people just dying to meet me," he recalled recently. He buried some of his friends and a few relatives. He closed the graves of his friends' children. He had a healthy respect for death and the dead, perhaps more than he had for some of the living.

But dead was dead, and seven acres of buffalo grass still needed to be mowed. Clipping around headstones and cedar trees with hand shears is what my mom, younger sister and I did. By junior high, though, I grew strong enough to take turns with Dad and dig that clay.

In the winter, the hilltop often was so frozen that he would need a pickax, and the summers were so hot he could dig only in the morning. "Sometimes in a dry year the ground was hard all the way down," Dad said.

We stood on one grave to dig a new one next door. Often we rested against a headstone. No disrespect was intended. As no skeletal hand grabbed our ankles at twilight, apparently none was taken.

"A lot of people keep from walking on graves, but I never had no rule, 'cause I used to stand on them myself. It all depends on how superstitious you are," Dad said.

We told jokes, many of them along the lines of having one foot already in the grave. Sometimes we inflicted death ourselves, plinking ground squirrels with a .22 bolt-action rifle because their burrows caught the mower's wheels and could pitch the rider into a stone. But Dad didn't allow ill to be spoken of the dead. And few things made him as angry as when high-school drivers turned disrespectful doughnuts in his grass.

The graves were at least six feet long, five feet deep and thirty-two inches wide, bigger if the family wanted a concrete vault to hold the coffin. Bolted-together boards laid atop the ground framed the hole-to-be. We sliced the sod with a narrow spade, then dug with garden shovels and heaved the dirt up onto plywood sheets next to the hole.

The next day, during the funeral, we sat at a distance and waited for the procession to glide out of the cemetery. The funeral home's man would strike the tent, roll up the green carpet and pack the mechanism that had lowered the coffin. Then I would ask Dad for permission to fill the grave. The grain shovel was big for me, but I pushed it along the plywood and over the hole. The first clods fell with a thunk against the coffin and filled in around the polished copper and within half an hour we were laying the flower sprays like a blanket on the mounded dirt.

We would be back in a few days to collect the wilted flowers for the rubbish pile. Our final ministration came after the next heavy rain, when we brought dirt in the pickup to fill in where the disturbed soil had settled. Eventually, the land would lie flat and the buffalo grass would grow again across the bare place.

Pawnee Rock Township paid Dad a sexton's wage. The fee for opening and closing a grave, usually about $30, was "paid by the ones left alive."

Now, twenty-five years later, graves in Pawnee Rock are dug with a backhoe, an efficient machine that scars the sod and never stains itself with tears. But the rules of human behavior in cemeteries are still the same, and they all revolve around respect.

∞

Etiquette tips

Consider these guidelines for cemetery etiquette:

- **Leave enough time to see the cemetery properly.** Park where you won't block traffic. Melvin Kerchee, Jr., manager of the Fort Sill, Oklahoma, cemeteries, says, "We have a sign at the Chiefs' Knoll that says, 'Do not block the roadway,' and people still stop right there."

- **Walk or don't walk on graves.** Some people mean no harm by strolling on graves; others feel better on "safe" ground. Respect for the dead aside, it's a matter of safety when the old wooden coffins rot away, and the ground above them won't support as much weight.

At the Alabama-Coushatta Cemetery in Polk County, Texas, a sign at the gate covers "about everything we ask" of visitors, says Sherman Williams, the caretaker. It reads: "Visitors are welcome on the reservation. If you enter our cemetery, don't touch or trample on graves. Thank you."

"Some of these graves have been there for years and years," Mr. Williams says. One day during a ceremony with a big crowd, "one of the graves just caved in."

- **Grave rubbings are generally OK, but be gentle.** Peg Smith, a member of the committee overseeing Mount Holly Cemetery in Little Rock, Arkansas, says, "We used to let anybody make rubbings, but somebody ruined a monument by using a ballpoint pen." Now the committee asks fans to know what they're doing. The best way is to use charcoal and butcher paper, and have someone else hold the paper.

At Fort Sill, Mr. Kerchee says grave rubbings are OK on the newer stones, but he wants visitors to contact the Fort Sill Museum before making them on older markers. "On real old stones, the rock facings have deteriorated so much that scratchings will deteriorate the stone."

- **Don't take things.** This should be obvious. "I don't think they should remove anything from the cemetery," says Mary Nell Turner, of the Rose Hill Cemetery Association in Hope, Arkansas. "Some people take a little dirt, but if everybody did that, there wouldn't be anything left, would there?"

- **Don't intrude on funeral services.** Be discreet during this important period in a family's life.

- **Ask permission before entering private land.** If you open a gate, close it.

- **Leave the grounds chaste and the wildlife unchased.**

"The only rule at Eureka Springs Cemetery is 'No dogs please,'" says Fred Hopkins, the Founders Cemetery plot salesman in the Arkansas town.

Support your local cemetery
Leon Unruh

Perhaps there's an old cemetery down the street or in a field you pass by. If you're interested in seeking historical status for it, the Texas Historical Commission can help.

The Austin-based agency has prepared a pamphlet—*Texas Preservation Guidelines: Preserving Historic Cemeteries*—and an application form. The booklet provides an overview of the preservation process, as well as of cemetery laws concerning dedication, access, abandonment and desecration. The form asks for a history of the cemetery, lists the documentation required, and asks for photographs. The form has specific questions about the ownership of the cemetery, the types of markers used, the landscaping, and the graveyard's cultural association, among other things. Examples are included.

To request the material, contact Gerron Hite, cemetery preservation coordinator, at

Local History Program

Texas Historical Commission

P.O. Box 12276

Austin 78711-2276

(512) 475-4167

e-mail: ghite@access.texas.gov

Texas

Scottsville—
A Favorite of Readers

Kathryn Straach

A twenty-five-foot statue of a Confederate soldier, honoring those who died in the Civil War, greets visitors to the Scottsville Cemetery, east of Marshall. But you might not even notice as your eyes dart from the magnificent statuary to the Grecian temples to the brownstone chapel.

The cemetery isn't large, but it is impressive. It was the burial place most often cited when *The Dallas Morning News* Travel section asked readers to name their favorite cemeteries in Texas and the neighboring states.

It was founded in 1841 by Colonel William Thomas "Buck" Scott, a newcomer from Mississippi, who started the town of Scottsville in 1834. He served in the Senate of the Republic of Texas and for eight terms in the Texas Legislature; he controlled five cotton plantations; and he supplied basic necessities to the Confederacy. He was married to Mary Washington Rose, daughter of William Pinckney Rose. The tall spire at Mr. Rose's grave in the cemetery states he was a soldier in the War of 1812, Hero at the Battle of New Orleans and Texas Pioneer. He also was known as an outlaw for his antics as a Regulator leader during the Regulator-Moderator War.

Mr. Scott's daughter Bettie and her husband, Pete Youree, built the brownstone chapel that sits in the northeast corner of the cemetery in 1904 in memory of their only son Will. Will's monument is a huge weeping angel with the epitaph, "If tears could have

Brownstone chapel, Scottsville Cemetery

saved you, thou would not have died."

A winding path leads to the plantation house and the family's original log cabin. A Methodist campground is behind the cemetery.

To get to the cemetery from Marshall, travel east on U.S. Highway 80 until it intersects with FM 1998. Travel east through Scottsville, just past the intersection of FM 2199; the cemetery is on the north side of the road.

Paris' Evergreen

Another impressive East Texas cemetery is Evergreen Cemetery in Paris, with lots of big trees and leaning tombstones that look as if they could use a good scrubbing. The cemetery had so many angels it was targeted a few years ago by a national theft ring.

Probably the best-known grave is that of Willet Babcock, who is more affectionately called Cowboy Jesus because his statuary has a Christ figure wearing cowboy boots.

"The man had a sense of humor," says Jim Blassingame, a third-generation cemetery caretaker. "That's just how he saw Jesus. Now, he'd probably have on Nikes."

The grave of D. H. Moore, owner of the White Elephant Saloon in Paris, is carved with skulls and doves and sabers and axes. "Everything cancels each other out," says Mr. Blassingame.

Also carved on it: "From Your Loving Wife, Marvin."

"Not too many women were named Marvin," says Mr. Blassingame, shaking his head.

"Cemeteries are places of history. That's all," he says. "They all had life, they had a history, they did things," he says, looking around him.

Some of the people buried in the cemetery aren't even from the area.

"It's just an old country cemetery," Mr. Blassingame says. "People like that." Some people passing through, even from other states, just decide that's where they want to be buried.

Near the back of the cemetery is a huge crypt patterned after that of actor Tyrone Powers. Larry Ford Ferguson, a big Tyrone fan, bought thirty-six grave spaces for his future resting spot and flew folks out to California to see Mr. Powers' grave in order to get the spot just right.

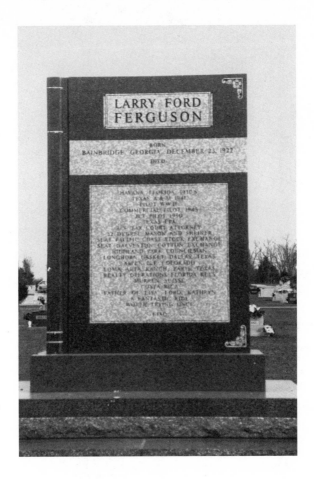

Diamond Bessie

Kathryn Straach

Bessie Moore, wife of a diamond salesman and better known as Diamond Bessie because of the jewels she wore, was murdered in 1876. She's buried in the Oakwood Cemetery in Jefferson, Texas. Every spring during the Jefferson Pilgrimage, the town performs the Diamond Bessie Murder Trial, which is a sellout.

Antagonists Robertson and Rose (first names unknown), who shot each other, lie in a common grave in Jefferson's Oakwood Cemetery. Two iron posts, chained together with no explanation, mark their grave.

A Tranquil Place in the Piney Woods

Leon Unruh

Colmesneil

Eighty miles straight south of Scottsville and a few hundred yards south of the Neches River near Colmesneil, a sand road heads west into the pine forest off U.S. Highway 69. County Road 2875 bobs and weaves for about a mile and a half, bright with puddles from the afternoon's violent storm, and ends at a farmhouse. I get out of my truck near the "Dog Will Bite" sign, intending to walk a hundred feet to a man standing over a blown-down pine.

"Get in your vehicle and drive over," he calls. "The dog will bite."

His directions send me through a cow pasture and back into the Piney Woods, where eventually a fallen tree blocks the track. On past a deer skeleton, I walk uphill in the dying light, until there they are: the stone grave houses of Sturrock Cemetery.

The Sturrock family left Scotland in the 1830s and settled in Tyler County, setting up a sawmill, gristmill and cotton gin at the mouth of Billums Creek and occasionally feuding with families in nearby Ogden. When the time came, the Sturrocks and their neighbors laid the dead in the ground and used sandstone rocks to build false crypts over them. The dozen crypts, perhaps four feet wide, nine feet long and three feet high, are said to resemble the style of houses the Sturrocks had in Scotland.

It is the most tranquil cemetery I have ever been in. The sun dapples the crypts and lone wooden grave

(left and below) The Sturrock family built false crypts that are said to resemble the buildings they left behind in Scotland.

A grave house covers the remains of J. Leonard Sturrock, 1919–1923.

house with a mellow light. The air is still; the only sounds come from mosquito wings and my footsteps on the grass.

In such a God's-country location, it is easy to feel the satisfaction suggested in a small marker at the crypt of Cynthia Sturrock (1819–53): "Citizen of the Republic of Texas."

Tyler County cemeteries have relatively standard markers that do not match the Sturrock style. Jack Whitmeyer, president of the Tyler County Genealogical Society, says, "As far as I know, for the county, that is probably the most unique." The genealogists have tracked down 107 white cemeteries and fewer than ten black cemeteries in the county, he says. Books locating the cemeteries and listing their occupants are kept at the genealogical society's library in Heritage Village, just west of Woodville on U.S. 190.

One cemetery, belonging to the Hall family, is known to exist, but where it is remains a question. "It's in a heavily timbered area, and there aren't any landmarks around it," Mr. Whitmeyer says. "We can draw a one-mile circle after it. . . . And there ain't nobody who can find where it is."

Some burial spots probably will never be found. In the early days of white settlement, when narrow wagon roads were first sliced through the forest, an old woman died and her family started to carry her to the family cemetery. But it had been raining and the wagon got stuck.

"They just buried her in a big cypress log by the wagon trail," Mr. Whitmeyer says. "They meant to go back and move her, but they never did."

Barnes and Noble Texans in Tyler County

Leon Unruh

Chester
Barnes

There's nothing shy about the Barneses of Chester in Tyler County. Large headstones and spires abound over their graves at Mount Hope Cemetery, and a sense of the founders and their descendants can be taken from their epitaphs.

In or shortly before 1836, the year of Texas' independence, James and Tabitha Huff Barnes moved to a hilltop in northwestern Tyler County in East Texas. When their daughter, Cynthia, died that year, they buried her in the yard as she had requested, making the first entry in what became Mount Hope Cemetery. As the years passed, the slave-holding Barnes family prospered in the blackland soil.

Chester is fifteen miles northwest of Woodville on U.S. 287. Mount Hope Cemetery is a little ways northeast of town on the road past the high school, but you will not find history this good in any high school text. On the Barnes mausoleum wall is a bit of history, concluding with a quotation from the occasion: "Here in James Barnes' home in 1839, during a camp meeting conducted by an English missionary from Europe, a collection was taken which started and built the Mt. Hope Methodist Church.

"In God we trust. Truly, this is God's 3.6 acres."

It is possible to let the tombstones tell the story. James and Tabitha Barnes, for example, are written up on what is known as the "history spire."

James Barnes died in 1863. His epitaph reads:

16

"Founded Mount Hope Church 1837. Laid out townsite of Jackson Miss 1820. A friend of the Indians. Loved by his family. Adored by his slaves. His mission—to establish schools and churches in the farthest reaches of civilization. Advice—Cultivate good soil. Observation—Honest labor is always rewarded."

Tabitha Huff Barnes died about the same time. Hers reads: "Born in Scotland during Revolutionary Period. Captured by the Indians and forced to dance the war dance under scalps of whites. Released through the friendship of husband and Indians. Died at Mount Hope 1863. Aggressive, modest pioneer that never shirked."

"It's all pretty well verified," says Jack Whitmeyer, president of the Tyler County Genealogical Society.

Tyler County was settled mostly by Southerners, and hundreds from the county fought for the Confederacy. Many stones announce armed service in the Confederate cause, but there is also one for Nancy E. Hopkins Barnes (1858–1931), six or seven years old when the war ended, but later the wife of a Confederate soldier: "A flower of Southern chivalry, a devoted mother, and an immaculate Christian."

Nearby lies Henry Clyde Fortenberry, who came into the world just a couple miles away in Peach Tree, which more or less dissolved when the railroad went south of town instead of through it in 1883. (The new settlement along the tracks was named after Chester A. Arthur, president from 1881 to 1885.) Fortenberry's epitaph: "Born at Peach Tree Village Tex. Sept 26, 1880. Died at the A. & M. College. College Station Tex. May 29, 1900."

And then there is the singular descendant Earl Huff Barnes:

 1.1.83 6.6.66
 I was the 1st. child
 1st. grandchild
 1st. great grandchild
 Born on the
 1st. Day of the Year
 1st. Day of the Month
 1st. Day of the Week
 Between 12 & 1 A.M.

Amid all the Barneses stands a row of enormous and bland stones from the Carnes family, merchants in town. Even there, however, the human touch survives in the form of a small white marker that remembers twenty-seven-year-old Anita Willene Carnes. Miss Carnes died after she was thrown from a horse: "Anita loves everybody and everybody seems to love her." And finally, there are husband and wife Bower Barnes (1884–1946) and Joe Roddy Barnes (1890): "They were real Texans who loved God and their family."

© Leon Unruh

"I Am at Rest"

A few miles southwest of Chester on Farm Road 1745 sits the Polk County hamlet of Barnes. This crossroads got its name in the late 1800s, says Mary Cryer, of the Mount Hope Cemetery Association, not strictly from the Barneses of Chester but because four families that lived there threw their names into a hat.

"The name they drew out would be the name of the community," she says. Beard, Handley and Havis stayed in the hat.

What makes the story unusual is that these Barneses evidently were, in the words of an early publication, "a highly respected Negro couple," and the rest of the families were white.

Many Barneses lie at Lilly Island Cemetery, a spot of red loam on the northeast outskirts of Barnes and just down the road from Lilly Island Church. Among them is Preston Wheatly Barnes (1890–1968): "Death leaves a shining mark."

The cemetery, still in use and splendid under a canopy of old cedars draped with Spanish moss, holds many people—not all of them Barneses—born in the slave-holding era and their children. As you wander across the broad lawn, look with empathy for the Freeman family stones and other proud markers such as these:

Mary Miller (1847–1911): "I am at rest."

The stone of Martin Luther Rigsby (1925–1946) carries a portrait of him in his Navy uniform.

Was Tyler First, Or Was Its Cemetery?

Tom Simmons

In 1846, John Lollar bought his brother Isaac's land grant and set aside five acres for a cemetery, called Lollar's. Tyler was established as a city April 11, 1846. You could call it a dead heat.

Lollar's became Oakwood Cemetery in 1903 when the city added some land. The oldest marker in the cemetery is that of P. M. Scott, born August 6, 1848, died September 3, 1852. Although the cemetery is still being used, graves are sometimes overgrown. If you brush aside a bit of grass, you will see a round marker about the size of a dinner plate, level with the ground, marking the four-year-old's burial site. There are eight other Scotts nearby.

Its 2,000-plus marked graves tell the story of the pioneers in this East Texas "rose capital of the world"— from a Hungarian count named Emir Hamvasy to a Texas governor, Richard B. Hubbard; a house servant, Cynthia Rabb; and a grouping of Jews. Count Hamvasy fled his homeland and became Tyler's first Episcopal rector; a street is named for him, but he does not loom large in the cemetery.

In fact, the first eye-catcher is a tall monument dedicated to Confederate soldiers, erected in 1907 by the United Daughters of the Confederacy (UDC). A Texas historical marker dated 1978 is nearby. Another prominent marker is the centerpiece of the Goodman family plot: a large Italian sculptured marble angel. It was erected by Dr. William J. Goodman after the death

Monument dedicated to Confederate soldiers

of his wife Priscilla in 1915. The cost was $2,000, and workmen used 300-pound cakes of ice to ensure that it would be placed exactly right, but how, we don't know.

There is nothing like the personal touch to stimulate cemetery browsers. My daughter, Susie Simmons Weir, and her children in Tyler are descendants of the Bowens who came from Culpeper, Virginia, after the Civil War and became prominent in Tyler life (and death) with headstones dating from 1876 to 1888. Susie moved from Dallas to Tyler in 1980, and she has now found traces of the early Bowens. Ten-year-old Jeffrey, sent to scout for Bowens, reported negative results. Then, a winner! The most famous Bowen was Nellie May Bowen Fields, and it was the Fields headstone and a UDC marker that drew his attention at first. Mrs. Fields lived in Dallas for many years and was a stirring leader of the UDC and the Dallas Southern Memorial Association. She moved to Tyler shortly before her death. Now Susie and Jeffrey identify with the Bowen plot, about fifteen by fifty feet—people they had never heard of. But it gives them a new sense of history.

Madge Ward of Tyler

Tom Simmons

Tyler •

Rose Hill is Tyler's second cemetery, its first burial being that of Assad John Sarkid, born in 1882 in Lebanon, died in Tyler in May 1917. Now the cemetery holds multimillionaires, politicians, paupers, veterans from the Civil War through Vietnam, people of distinction and average folks, as it sits on Tyler's north-south lifeline, Broadway, not far from downtown.

Its most impressive monument is that of Madge Ward, a pianist of great talent, who entertained generations of music lovers in this country and overseas. She taught in Tyler schools, entertained troops at Camp Fannin in World War II, and performed her one-woman show at dinner clubs, hotels and resorts, and on cruise ships and the airwaves. What better gravestone than a more-than-life-size grand piano, eight feet tall and thirteen feet long, created at her request out of Canadian marble. Entering Tyler's Rose Hill Cemetery from Donnybrook, a visitor's view of this site is impressive. It sits alone, a few unrelated gravestones nearby, right by the road. Nobody's likely to steal it—it weighs twenty-five tons, plus twelve tons of concrete in the foundation. In death, she is still a show-stopper. Her casket is under the piano legs. The simple inscription is "Madge Ward / Aug. 22, 1911–May 4, 1995."

Few family plots anywhere will be more eye-catching than that of the Zwans, whose oldest members came from Lebanon. A dozen gravestones line the curving roadside not far from the grand piano,

but not all of them have graves. Three have saucer-sized pictures: "Michael Anthony Zwan, Dec. 12, 1917–May 5, 1995, Father of Tanya, With life and name unstained, a good man dies"; "Tanya Michele Zwan, June 22, 1962– Oct. 3, 1995, Trailing clouds of glory as she came too splendid for this world. This world was never meant for one as beautiful as you. May love's happy journey take you to the most magnificent places"; and "Carol Ann McBride Zwan, Mar. 8, 1934 / Mother of Tanya."

Carol Zwan answers the phone; Mike and Tanya are still listed in the telephone book. Does this bother you, the picture and all? I ask.

"No, I put it there myself," she says. As others in the family move on, there will be places for them.

Rose Hill is keeping up with the times; a mausoleum is being added on the Broadway side. A few family mausoleums dot the cemetery.

And a cemetery must have mysteries. Howard Pollan, Rose Hill historian, wrote that rumor has it that some of the old horses used by the Tyler Fire Department were buried here. When Wilma Street was being cut through, bones much too large for a human were uncovered. That mystery may never be solved.

In 1982 the East Texas Genealogical Society published a complete list of graves in Oakwood, just west of downtown, and Rose Hill, on South

Broadway, and the graves' approximate locations. The Oakwood-Rose Hill book can be bought at the Tyler Library, 201 S. College, for $15; ask in the third-floor genealogical department.

In New London, Many Graves Bear Same Date

Kathryn Straach

New • London

"Happy and gay to school our little boy went one day. He never returned but we thank God. He is not dead, just away."

That's the epitaph on the tombstone of Curtis Reams. And Winnifred Melvene Drake, and several others who died in a tragic schoolhouse explosion in London, Texas, March 18, 1937. The explosion, caused by leaking natural gas that accumulated under the building, still ranks as the worst school disaster in U.S. history. One hundred and twelve of the approximately 300 students and teachers who died in that explosion are buried at Pleasant Hill Cemetery, about

four miles southeast of town. Although it's not even half the number who died, it's the final resting place for the largest number of victims buried in the same location.

At the time of the explosion, London, southeast of Tyler, was a booming oil town, and the school district was said to have been the richest in the country. But many of the students' families were transient oil workers, and many left in the days following the explosion. (The town was called London until a new post office opened in 1938. Because there already was a town by that name, it began calling itself New London.) The victims' graves are scattered throughout the nondescript cemetery that sits along State Highway 323. But even a visitor who doesn't take the time to read the historical marker at the cemetery entrance will realize something out of the ordinary happened in this town.

Many of the markers read, "Victim of the London School Disaster." Virginia Loe's states, "She was the sunshine in our home." Other markers are more generic, such as "Asleep in Jesus" or "Gone But Not Forgotten." Several of the tombstones have photos of the young victims smiling expectantly.

And then that date—March 18, 1937—is etched on tombstone after tombstone. The repetition chills the bones.

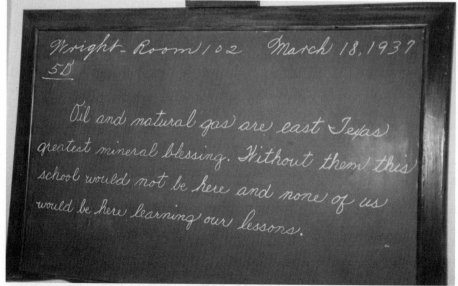

A New London museum detailing the town's explosion re-creates a chalkboard from the school on the day of the tragedy.

More than sixty years later, the tragedy still hangs over the town. A cenotaph, or empty tomb, sits on the street's median in front of the rebuilt school in honor of those who died. And just recently a new museum (featured in *The Dallas Morning News* Travel section, April 5, 1998) detailing the explosion opened.

Hoss Rests on Range in De Kalb

Kathryn Straach

De Kalb

Dan Blocker may have been bigger than life itself as he rode across the Ponderosa in the popular TV series *Bonanza.* For fourteen years, the burly Mr. Blocker rode into our living rooms as Hoss Cartwright. But there is a mere nod to his fame at the Woodmen Cemetery, where he is buried in De Kalb in far-northeast Texas. A quick drive through the cemetery that sits along U.S. Highway 82 gives no indication such a big star is buried here. Mr. Blocker's grave looks no different from everyone else's.

The family plot has a Blocker headstone, and to the right on the ground is a marker that merely reads: "B. Dan D. Blocker, Dec. 10, 1928 May 13, 1972." You'd think the word "Hoss" would be etched somewhere on the stone. The only allowance that someone special is in this cemetery is on the map at the entrance: One of the roads is named Blocker Drive; the other roads have generic names such as Memorial, Heavenly, Angel and Peaceful.

Although some of the headstones in the cemetery date to the 1800s, the cemetery has that relatively new look, with shiny marble headstones all about the same size, and very few trees. Breaking the monotony are the tall Woodmen of the World markers, and cattle grazing on the land surrounding the cemetery.

The De Kalb grave of Dan Blocker, a.k.a. Hoss Cartwright on TV's Bonanza, *is unpretentious.*

Shells, Bears Mark American Indian graves

Leon Unruh

Indian Reservation

At the Alabama-Coushatta Indian Reservation, the sun, even at midday, accentuates the molded soil on top of the graves. The mounds of some families are bare. Others carry decorations: seashells, coffee cups, stones, a ceramic swan in a frying pan. Erosion has stranded some decorations atop tiny pillars of dirt. An infant's grave, decorated the modern way with a teddy-bear-shaped stone, has a traditional southern scraped plot (bare earth with all vegetation removed).

© Leon Unruh

A ceramic swan in a frying pan decorates this grave.

The tribal cemetery sprawls next to the Presbyterian mission, a white frame reminder of the Indians' long struggle. Among the graves are those of chiefs and elders who guided the tribes through difficult periods in the Piney Woods.

The Alabamas and Coushattas arrived in East Texas before the War for Independence and settled for good in Polk County in the 1850s on a reservation granted them as a reward for not siding with Mexico during the war. Fortune changed for the tribes after the Civil War, however, when white settlers' misanthropy and federal and state indifference left the tribes with almost nothing. But in the early 1880s, according to *The New Handbook of Texas*, the Presbyterians, railroad and timber mills arrived, providing some educational and economic opportunities. Finally, in 1924, the government recorded them as citizens.

Some tribal traditions have survived—a craft store at the reservation entrance along U.S. 190 sells handcrafts—but Sherman Williams, the caretaker of the cedar-shaded graveyard, says there is no strict burial tradition.

"We put up mounds if the family asks," he says. "They place all those cups on top of the graves. They say the spirit uses them on their journey."

Many markers are humble. Leaders have large stones, generally with detailed inscriptions of their service to the tribes. Chiefs include John Scott, 1805–1913, who served in the Confederate Army and came to Texas in the 1880s. He has a Confederate memorial. Sub-Chief Colabe Sylestine was a co-signer of the land grant received by the Alabamas and helped during the move of 1852. And there's Robert Fulton Battise—Chief Kina of the Bear Clan—who was born on the reservation in 1909, grew up in a one-room log cabin and earned money cutting wood for the railroad. He became second chief in 1936 and principal chief in 1970, a ceremonial position, but one he used to push for the development of tourism, hous-

Neatly shaped mounds

© Leon Unruh

ing construction, a Head Start program, and a medical clinic. He died in 1994; his grave marker lists his line of ancestry.

Rural cemeteries

Follow FM 2500, then FM 942 and FM 1745 north from the reservation for a look at some rural cemeteries. Keep your eye open for small signs announcing that a cemetery is down a dirt road. In addition, the Polk County Museum, 514 W. Mill Street in Livingston, sells *Cemeteries in Polk County, Texas*, an inexpensive booklet that locates 140 county cemeteries.

- Usher—Usher Cemetery, a scraped cemetery, has several Confederate veterans and their families. Turn off the paved road at the Usher Cemetery sign just north of the reservation water tower. Follow a sand road for four-tenths of a mile, then turn left and go another four-tenths through the clear-cut forest. Trees remain around the cemetery. Watch out during deer season; hunters' stands are all around.
- Feagin—On April 25, 1998, Harleyne Clamon, chairwoman of the Polk County Historical Commission, dedicated a state historical marker at Feagin Cemetery. "My mother's father's people are the ones who made all this come about" when they moved from Alabama in the 1850s, she says. Great-great-grandfather Aaron Feagin bought 2,800 acres in the area with a $10,000 gold piece. The patriarch donated the land for the cemetery (the family also provided for Parrish Cemetery near Hortense on FM 942). Feagin Cemetery, on Clamon Country Road, has more than 200 graves, including some unmarked sites. An apparently unnamed black cemetery is west from Feagin Cemetery. It is a small cleared spot with a handful of markers.
- Nowlin—Nowlin Cemetery has another traditional form of decoration: grave houses. These large wooden structures have fence walls and cover three graves; at most other cemeteries they cover only one. The stones here date from 1907. Take Caney Loop off FM 1745, driving a mile until you pass the church. Turn at the cemetery sign and follow a dirt road three-tenths of a mile east.

Texas Inmates and Heroes Are Laid to Rest in Huntsville

Kathryn Straach

Huntsville •

Cold metal bars no longer restrain the prisoners in this state correctional town—at least not in their final resting places. Captain Joe Byrd Memorial Cemetery lies on open land. There are no fences and gates. No lockup ever. People are free to come and go twenty-four hours a day. More than 1,700 prisoners unclaimed at the time of their deaths are buried in the twenty-two-acre prison cemetery on the border of Sam Houston State University.

Graves are marked with only inmates' numbers and death dates.

The land for the prison cemetery was deeded to the state in 1885, but prisoners have been buried here since shortly after the establishment of the state penal system in 1848. The earliest decipherable marker is dated 1870.

No one is certain how many graves exist because early graves were marked with wooden crosses that later rotted, and the thicket was so heavy with underbrush many graves were lost. Wooden crosses were eventually replaced with rectangular headstones with the prisoner's name and number until those markers started disappearing. (Not to point fingers, but Huntsville *is* a college town.) Now prisoners' graves are marked with only their number carved into a simple concrete cross.

The cemetery is named for a veteran prison employee who took it upon himself to clear and beautify the place of dense foliage. Captain Joe Byrd asked for inmate labor to help him, and it is still maintained that way. Of the prisoners buried here, more than 200 were executed. Some died while trying to escape; some were killed by fellow inmates; others perished of natural causes. Many died of the flu during a World War I epidemic—when the cemetery's only four women were buried.

In the middle of the cemetery is a monument to Chief Satanta, a Kiowa Indian chieftain convicted of killing seven settlers during the 1871 Salt Creek Massacre. He committed suicide in 1878 by jumping from a window of the penitentiary. It took the Kiowa tribe eighty-five years before successfully getting his body moved to Fort Sill, Oklahoma, where, in 1963, 2,000 Kiowas honored their lost leader. (See also pp. 140–144.)

In 1993, prison officials chopped down more than 250 pines because the trees created so much shade grass wouldn't grow, leaving the soil vulnerable to erosion. The hatchet job practically caused a riot among conservationists, as well as others who just liked the parklike beauty of the trees. Now the cemetery looks nearly barren, bordered by a mobile-home park on one side, a car wash and mini-warehouse on another.

∞

Sam Houston and Friends

The trees are still dense at Oakwood Cemetery across town, where Sam Houston and other Texas heroes are buried. Having served as a U.S. senator and governor of two states and as first president of the Republic of Texas, the controversial and colorful leader died July 26, 1863, of pneumonia.

He is buried, at his request, near good friend Henderson Yoakum, as well as other good friends, Thomas Gibbs, Thomas Carothers, J. Carol Smith and Anthony Branch. On the seventy-fifth anniversary of the Battle of San Jacinto, the state erected a monument at his grave. (See photo above.) Sculpted by Pompeo Coppini, the monument depicts Houston as the general in command of the Texas Army. On the left is Lady Victory and on the right is Lady History. The torches on the monument, as well as the axes on the wrought-iron fence surrounding his grave, are inverted, symbolizing Peace.

In the middle of the cemetery is a strip of land—measuring the full distance of the cemetery's north and south boundaries—reserved for African-Americans. Many slaves are buried here in unmarked graves.

The cemetery is full of historic figures: thirty-two are detailed in a walking-tour brochure put out by the Huntsville Tourism Council and Huntsville/Walker County Chamber of Commerce (409) 295-8813. Stop by the chamber, just blocks from the cemetery, for a copy.

A few of the notables buried here include Jane Ward, a freed slave best remembered as the organizer of the Juneteenth Celebration on Emancipation Day, and Joshua Houston, Sam Houston's body servant, whose story is told in *From Slave to Statesman: The Legacy of Joshua Houston, Servant to Sam Houston*.

Don't miss the grave of Rawley Rather Powell, who died at the age of five. His parents bought a large wooded tract to the north of Oakwood Cemetery and dedicated it as a wildwood sanctuary. A large bronze statue of Christ, sculpted by Bertel Thorwaldsen, overlooks his grave. The original is in Copenhagen.

Gardenlike Glenwood Only One of Houston and Galveston's Sites

Kathryn Straach

Houston

Galveston

Glenwood in Houston is the 90210 of cemeteries.

The lush, hilly parklike cemetery with striking views of skyscrapers in the background is the coveted final address for some of Houston's most prominent—from Republic of Texas president Anson Jones to billionaire Howard Hughes.

Northwest of downtown, Glenwood covers sixty-four rolling acres with winding roads overlooking Buffalo Bayou. Huge oaks and pines tower over the elaborate marble statuary in the older section of the cemetery. Plots in the newer section are merely bricked-off, perfectly manicured lawn areas, some with park benches.

But don't count on stumbling upon Howard Hughes' grave. He is nearly as elusive in death as in life. His grave is elevated off the street, with steps leading up to it, and enclosed in a locked light-green wrought-iron fence. The marker is flush with the ground and is not visible from the street. A curved concrete wall behind the graves of Howard and his parents is the only decorative feature other than bright yellow flowers and green grass.

But don't leave after tracking down the eccentric billionaire's grave. Drive every windy road here because every curve offers a new vista. Take time to

Howard Hughes' grave

discover this cemetery's diversity, all of which is stunning. In the center is the caretaker's office, an unusual German gingerbread-style house. The cemetery is at 2525 Washington Blvd.

A Murder Took Rice

Also in Houston is the grave of William Marsh Rice. His remains can be found in the center of the neatly manicured Rice University campus. A 2,000-pound bronze statue of the school's founder rests atop a granite base containing an urn with Mr. Rice's remains. Mr. Rice was murdered by his valet and companion Charles Jones, who had conspired with attorney Albert Patrick to acquire the Rice estate.

William Marsh Rice

Isle's Grand Graves

Less than an hour to the southeast is Galveston, with its New Orleans-style cemeteries—plural—along Broadway. Although the graves from 40th through 43rd Streets look like one big burial ground, they are actually in seven different cemeteries. A road cuts between 40th and 43rd with grave-yards on both sides.

Here you will find Old City Cemetery, containing 2,895 grave sites; Oleander Cemetery, also known as Old Potter's Field; Evergreen Cemetery; New City Cemetery, also called the Fever Yard; Hebrew Benevolent Society Cemetery; Old Catholic Cemetery; and Trinity Episcopal Cemetery.

The Galveston Historical Foundation used to issue a booklet with a little history on each and some of the interesting individuals buried here. Now the foundation offers a tour each January or February—usually the Sunday after the Super Bowl—of the town's sacred sites, including the cemeteries. Call (409) 765-7834.

The cemeteries are filled with historical characters, including Michel Menard, signer of the Texas Declaration of Independence; Thomas Henry Borden, part of Stephen F. Austin's "Old 300"; and Captain Aaron Burns, who delivered the Twin Sisters (pieces of artillery) to Sam Houston during the Texas Revolution. A marker mentions George Campbell Childress, co-author and signer of the Texas Declaration of Independence and creator of

One of the seven cemeteries along Broadway in Galveston

A mausoleum in one of Galveston's cemeteries

the Lone Star symbol, although he is buried on the present site of a Galveston school.

One of the most interesting stories is that of the Perugini brothers, Frank and Tony, born on the same date two years apart. Not knowing what the other was doing, they joined the Navy in separate states on the same day. And they died on the same day in a torpedo gun turret on the cruiser *New Orleans* during the Battle of the Solomons in World War II. Now they are buried together in Galveston's Old Catholic Cemetery.

Houston Museum
Puts the "Fun" in Funerals

Kathryn Straach

Houston

Here is a to-die-for attraction: The National Museum of Funeral History, formerly the American Funeral Service Museum, the largest of its kind in North America.

In far north Houston, the museum opened in 1992 to educate the public about the mysterious rituals associated with death, as well as to preserve funerary artifacts from the nineteenth and twentieth centuries. The exhibit area is more than 21,000 square feet in the west end of a building that also houses a mortuary college and funeral training classes.

The huge room is filled with a fleet of funeral-service vehicles, such as horse-drawn hearses, a

funeral sleigh and a Japanese ceremonial hearse. The latter is a modified 1972 Toyota Crown Station Wagon, with an ornate roof covered in copper and an interior painted with flowers and other designs. A massive 1916 Packard funeral bus, designed to replace the funeral procession, is also on display. It could carry a casket, pallbearers and twenty mourners. Unfortunately, the short-lived bus tipped backward while climbing a hill in San Francisco, and the pallbearers tumbled over the mourners, and the casket turned over. You will also find an ornate carriage used in the movie *Cyrano de Bergerac*.

But you will see much more than hearses. The historic aspects of funerals are explained in three short videos, and the exhibits lining the walls bring the funeral business to life, so to speak. The Funerals of the Famous Gallery displays artifacts related to a variety of celebrities and politicians such as John F. Kennedy, Elvis, Martin Luther King, Jr., and Judy Garland. Memorabilia from Abraham Lincoln's funeral is displayed, including a model of the train procession and a replica of his coffin. The exhibit includes a Secret Service book detailing the events of Lincoln's assassination and the search for suspect John Wilkes Booth.

The museum also features a re-created embalming room from the late 1920s and a display of embalming instruments and drainage tubes. You will also find burial clothing, door badges and mourning items, including a doll, fan, parasol and hatpin.

And, of course, there are coffins, from the very plain to fantasy versions crafted by Ghanian Kane Quaye, including those shaped like a fish eagle, a crab, a bull, a fishing canoe, a lobster, a leopard, a chicken, a Mercedes-Benz automobile, a Yamaha outboard motor, a fish and a shallot.

Probably even stranger than the fantasy coffins is the casket built for three. In the 1930s, a couple's small child died, and they were so distraught they planned for the husband to murder his wife, then commit suicide. Here is where the story gets really weird: The couple explained their plans to a funeral-home owner who specially made the casket. No questions asked? No calls made to the authorities? The couple changed their minds at the last minute, however.

And as at most museums, you can buy gift items. Don't forget friends and family with mugs or glasses, golf balls, pen sets or even watches adorned with a hearse. All you have to do is dig a little—into your pocket.

Fantasy coffins crafted by Ghanian Kane Quaye

To get there, exit West Richey off Interstate 45. Travel west on Richey, left on Ella, then left onto Barren Springs Drive; the address is 415. The museum is open daily, Monday through Friday, 10 A.M. to 4 P.M., and Saturday and Sunday, noon to 4 P.M. Admission is $5 ($3 for ages 3 to 12 and over 54). Call (281) 876-3063.

Birdhouses Help Save Chappell Hill Grounds

Kathryn Straach

Chappell Hill •

A retired oilman from Houston is responsible for breathing life into the Historic Chappell Hill Masonic Cemetery. Wayne Hesterly, who moved with his wife to Chappell Hill, was appalled when he saw the condition of the local Masonic Cemetery, final resting place of the immediate family of Colonel William Barret Travis, relatives of Davy Crockett, twenty-eight Confederate veterans and other historic characters.

"It was a jungle," he says.

In 1965, the Masonic Lodge had deeded the property to the community, and seventeen years later, the maintenance was abandoned altogether.

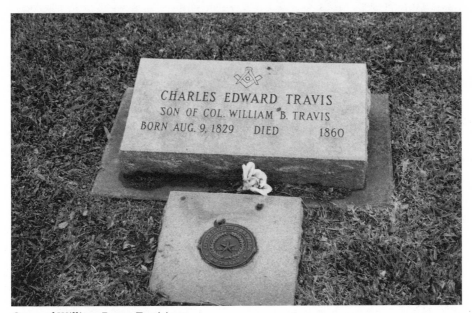

Grave of William Barret Travis' son

"Not only was it sad, but it was a disgrace," he says. He went to the local historical society, saying it needed to be restored, but "there was no interest in that old thing," he says, shaking his head.

"Our absolute world and heritage is in that cemetery."

So Mr. Hesterly, a Mason, lovingly took on the project himself. After a couple of years of hanging out in the cemetery, picking up debris, Mr. Hesterly was unanimously named president of the cemetery board by the three remaining members. Not that the official title made a lot of difference. He already was a whirlwind of dedication. Using $6,000 of a $20,000 endowment fund left by a local family, Mr. Hesterly bought a tractor to help clear roads. He drilled a well and cut down trash trees, replacing them with 100 cedars along the fence line and forty-five live oaks within the cemetery.

Not only did he physically restore the cemetery, but he also worked to ensure its financial future. One of his first projects was building birdhouses, which he sold at Chappell Hill's bluebonnet festival in the spring, and the scarecrow festival in the fall.

"When everyone in Washington County had two birdhouses, I started decorating gourds," he says.

He also added to the endowment fund by clearing an unused acre of cemetery land and selling cemetery plots. Two-thirds of the new area has been sold. That includes a plot for himself and his wife, who died in 1997. He added another $15,000 to the endowment by repairing tombstones for local people. And he has plans of publishing a book of his poems. Proceeds, of course, will go to the endowment fund. Officially, the cemetery restoration was complete in 1995, but Mr. Hesterly still has a few more plans, including a fountain and a large map.

Mr. Hesterly also is known for carrying out one of William Barret Travis' last wishes. In a final letter to a friend before he was killed at the Alamo, Colonel Travis asked for the continued care of his son Charles. Charles was reared by David Ayres and was buried in the Chappell Hill cemetery with other Travis relatives, but his grave never had a marker—that is, not until Mr. Hesterly bought one a few years ago. The heroic commander of the Alamo probably never imagined that his son ultimately would be cared for with funds collected from birdhouse sales.

The cemetery is .7 mile off FM 2447, which intersects with Main Street (FM 1155).

Terrell Needs a Guardian Angel

Jean Simmons

Terrell •

Oakwood Memorial Park, which lies along U.S. Highway 80 in a commercial area of Terrell, represents the height of turn-of-the-century tombstone ornamentation through its numerous large angels, obelisks, portrait sculptures and intricate stonework.

It also represents the dreadful loss that can occur from thievery, a universal problem. As recently as 1995–1997, a wrought-iron bench, angel statues from graves of little children, marble urns, and iron fencing were taken from Oakwood. What once was a suggested tour of six delicate angel statues on tombstones of children who died around 1900 has shrunk to just one, on the grave of John Drake Muckleroy. These pieces, as well as those from other East Texas cemeteries, were destined to wind up in malls and antique shops as valuable items.

Through the persistence of one sixth-generation Terrell resident, preservationist Davis Griffith-Cox, thievery has been stopped and many items have been returned, but

A remaining angel at Oakwood Memorial Park

no one has been sent to jail. Several suspects have fled the state.

Cemeteries in Forney, Mabank and Paris were also looted. Mr. Griffith-Cox found some of the items in Dallas on Lovers Lane and Henderson Avenue and they were returned.

But Oakwood has many remaining graves and monuments that will make a visit rewarding:

- A group of twenty tombstones marking the graves of RAF trainees killed at the British Flight Training School in Terrell during World War II.

- The grave of an early mayor, Matthew Cartwright, said to be the work of John Gutzon Borglum before he completed Mount Rushmore.

- A flat tombstone with a Texas historical marker over the burial site of western artist Frank Reaugh.

- A statue of General John S. Griffith, a Confederate cavalry commander, done by the Teich Studio of San Antonio; the grave of Robert Terrell, eponym of the city; the beautiful Carter angel, presumably writing in a book of life; a portrait sculpture of Helen Grinnan; and the 1992 grave of Netta Lavinia Griffith Cox, designed by restorationist Davis Griffith-Cox, who used both old and new materials to design his mother's grave to be compatible with older graves around it.

A leaflet that outlines a self-guided tour of the park can be picked up at the Terrell Visitors Center at Tanger Center. But bear in mind the text was written a few years ago, before the rash of thefts.

Graves Reveal Dallas' Parade of History

Leon Unruh

Dallas •

Dallas has a wealth of notable cemeteries with fascinating stories to tell. At rest under the live oaks are pioneers, politicians, developers, sports heroes, captains of industry, the venal and valiant. Among them:

Oakland

Once it was Dallas' crowning glory: Oakland Cemetery, full of pomp and artistry in the city's finest neighborhood south of the Trinity River. J. F. Strickland, who founded the company that became TU Electric, lies under a tall obelisk in the center of the cemetery. John Armstrong, developer of the suburb of Highland Park, is watched over by a towering, gossamer-clad marble angel imported from Venice. The Belo newspaper family is remembered with a pale stone slab and a cross. The Caruths, whose family owned much of what became North Dallas, have a columned monument.

Other families provided a legacy: Keist, Growler, O'Connor, Ervay, Record, Beall. There are such personages as Confed-

© Leon Unruh

erate General Richard M. Gano, who became a prohibitionist minister and the grandfather of eccentric millionaire Howard Hughes. But their funerals occurred decades ago, before the wealthy left their dead and moved north of the river. Now, these fifty acres seem to be on a Faulknerian slide back to nature, shrubs and wildflowers welcoming the hand-carved works into their grasp.

It is not for lack of effort by the live-in manager, Harold Williams, who works on a bare-bones budget to maintain the lovely old park in the 3900 block of Malcolm X Avenue in South Dallas. His office is an organized

Doves atop the Whitehurst monument in Oakland

mess of records, tools, bronze markers and the three-foot-tall "Bunny Boy" statue depicting young Joseph Milton Cary, who drowned in 1901. The statue, which originally stood at Joseph's grave, is kept inside for safekeeping from vandals and thieves.

Mr. Williams is a gregarious fellow who gladly provides background on people buried during the cemetery's first century. One of the favorite stories he and Dallas cemetery preservationist Frances James like to tell is about Louis Antonio Pires.

Mr. Pires arrived in this country as an orphan, says Mrs. James, his parents having died on the crossing from Portugal. He amassed a fortune in the utility business, lived in a Salvation Army home, never married, and left $500,000 to Buckner Children's Home. "He was old and sick, and his friends wanted him to go to the hospital, but he didn't want to go because he didn't want to spend the money," she says. In recognition, other families built him a monument for his grave. It has six columns and a dome, with inscriptions inside and out. The floor is inlaid with colored stone.

The floor of Louis Antonio Pires' monument

Burials continue at Oakland Cemetery, but the newer plot sizes and headstones are modest. Just before Memorial Day, octogenarian John Torres putters around a little plot with his shears.

"My mother is over there. See those red flowers?" he says. "And my wife is down that road, all the way, then on the left."

His friends, the Valdezes, died in a car wreck in 1978. Mr. Torres cares for their small concrete marker with its painted lettering because, he says, "They ain't got nobody to come."

Oak Cliff

When infant Martha White died in 1844, she was buried in a newly set-aside piece of land on Hord's Ridge, the original name for Oak Cliff. She may not have been the first person buried in what is now known as Oak Cliff Cemetery, which is along Eighth Street a few blocks east of R. L. Thornton Freeway (Interstate 35), but her grave has the distinction of being the oldest in Dallas with a marker.

Although time has made the writing hard to read, the stone is easy to find. Look for a white marker at the base of an enormous slanting oak tree along the western fence where it jogs outward. William Hord, for whom the ridge was named, is buried in Oak Cliff Cemetery, but his grave is unmarked, says David Eisenlohr, a member of the cemetery's board of trustees and relative of pioneer landscape painter Edward Gustav Eisenlohr, who also is here. Sam Houston's brother, William Rogers Houston, rests here, as do Oak Cliff developer Leslie Stemmons, mayors George Sergeant and George Sprague, and drugstore founder J. A. Skillern.

Anthony Boswell has a family plot in the back of the cemetery. A black teamster, he was an important landowner in Oak Cliff's historic Tenth Street area. Anthony and Boswell streets are named for him.

Beeman

John Neely Bryan opened his trading post along the Trinity River in 1841, five years after the Republic of Texas was born. He talked the John Beeman family into moving to the Dallas area (near White Rock Creek south of the present Interstate 30) and married their daughter, Margaret. Mr. Bryan eventually became insane and died at an asylum in Austin. The Beemans' graves are in their family cemetery behind a wire fence wrapped in mustang grapevines.

The Beemans, Cumbys and other neighbors can be visited by turning off Dolphin Road onto Mingo (at the African Methodist Episcopal Church), then Galt and Osage. It is behind Shearith Israel Cemetery.

© Leon Unruh

Beeman monument reads: "Mrs. Emily Beeman holding her son Scott and guarding against Indians in Dallas Co. in 1841."

*Grave of
Viola
Cumby*

Greenwood

Genteel old Greenwood Cemetery at 3020 Oak Grove Avenue in central Dallas has a rarity: a new hand-carved marble statue. Ruth Marie Rose was the godmother of State District Judge John M. Marshall's children when she died of cancer in 1987. She was buried in his family plot; as a final gift, Judge Marshall arranged for a statue to be produced in Italy.

"There was some guy over there with a chisel working on this thing for a year," he says.

The angel fits in nicely with the rich statuary of Greenwood, an 1875-vintage graveyard that originally was named Trinity Cemetery. Numerous obelisks and tall monuments were erected during the nineteenth century. Among the Dallas notables buried here are the Cockrells, who owned much of Dallas at one time and are the family for whom the burg of Cockrell Hill is named; developer John Cole; banker W. H. Gaston; and Christopher Columbus Slaughter, cattle king, Texas Ranger, and member of the expedition that took Cynthia Ann Parker back from the Comanches.

The trees and monuments provide such a classic setting that the television series *Walker, Texas Ranger* films its cemetery scenes under the tall oaks.

"The cemetery is really a historical site as much as anything else," Judge Marshall says.

© Leon Unruh

Greenwood Cemetery

Numerous Civil War veterans are here, too. For soldiers without a military headstone, the white tablet stones of the type found in national cemeteries are requested from the government as details about their federal or Confederate service are confirmed. Despite Greenwood's age, only forty percent of the grave sites have been sold, Judge Marshall says. Although anybody can apply for a plot here, it helps their cause if the applicants have a family member in place.

"We are in the business of being a historical monument here, and we don't want drug dealers in with respectable people," Judge Marshall says. "These people are all related to each other, so it's a family cemetery."

Grove Hill

© Leon Unruh

Cochran Tower, Grove Hill

Grove Hill Cemetery, at 4118 Samuell Boulevard in East Dallas, is an ornate treasure-trove of post-pioneer Dallasites: Tenison, Stemmons, Murdock, Munger, Genaro, Hubbard, Buckner. The names on the bulky tombstones and mausoleums—this must be one of the grandest collections of granite in Texas—also show up on roads, parks, lakes and children's homes around town.

But according to people in the cemetery office, the graves most sought by visitors are those of Dallas' star-crossed ring royalty. Professional wrestler

© Leon Unruh

Fritz von Erich, born Jack Adkisson, Sr., as well as a brother, a six-year-old son and his four wrestler sons lie in a humble area just east of the cross-shaped hedge marking out the Hilltop area. His four wrestling sons—David, Michael, Chris and Kerry—all died young, three of suicide, between 1984 and 1993. Fritz von Erich, who died of brain cancer in 1997, survived them all. He shares a marker with Kerry.

Grove Hill also has at least one Medal of Honor winner: Turney Leonard, a first lieutenant who fought the Germans during World War II.

© Leon Unruh

Laurel Land

Laurel Land Memorial Park has at least two legends. The grave of musician Stephen "Stevie" Ray Vaughan, who died in a Wisconsin helicopter crash in 1990, is on an island at the sprawling cemetery along South R. L. Thornton Freeway in Oak Cliff. It is on an east-west road near the Marsalis Avenue entrance. In the Laurel Land Mausoleum, not too far away from the man with the smokin' guitar, is barbecue king Sonny Bryan. The cemetery also is home to J. D. Tippet, the police officer slain in Oak Cliff by Lee Harvey Oswald on November 22, 1963, after President John F. Kennedy was shot.

© Leon Unruh

(left) Statuary at Laurel Land
(below) "Stevie" Ray Vaughan's monument

STEPHEN
RAY
VAUGHAN

OCTOBER 3   AUGUST 27
1954   1990

THANK YOU...
FOR ALL THE LOVE
YOU PASSED OUR WAY

© Leon Unruh

Pioneer

A stroll through this small cemetery just north of the Dallas Convention Center and adjacent to the longhorn statues reveals the origins of many of the city's street names: Young, Record, Peak, Harwood, Good. The roster also lists Juliette Fowler, who created a home for the elderly and for troubled youths; several judges; members of the Texas Congress; James Weck Latimer, the city's first newspaper publisher (of the *Cedar Snag* in 1848); and the Reverend William C. Young, the initial minister of what is now First United Methodist Church of Dallas.

The city's Confederate monument faces south at the edge of the cemetery next to the Convention Center. The cemetery used to be much larger, but many of the dead were moved to other cemeteries when the meeting hall was expanded in 1959.

Freedman's

Dallas' most historic black cemetery is Freedman's Cemetery, at Lemmon Avenue and Central Expressway north of downtown. Many of the city's early black residents were buried in this five-acre graveyard between 1861 and 1925. Although the site appears vacant from the street, as many as 10,000 people are thought to be buried there. Highway excavation crews unearthed some graves in the 1980s, and about 1,500 were dug up to make way for construction. They were reinterred nearby, and the city in 1999 dedicated an arch to commemorate the freedmen's lives. A few stones remain, huddled next to a wooded lot along the western fence. The script on one stone reads: "How much of light / How much of joy / Is buried with a darling boy."

Lincoln

Lincoln Memorial Park, a spacious area at 1311 Murdock Road in the Pleasant Grove area of southeast Dallas, is the city's principal black cemetery now. About seventy-five percent of the city's black burials are held there, *Dallas Morning News* columnist Norma Adams Wade reported in 1990. The cemetery opened in 1924. Listed among the buried are philanthropist Pearl C. Anderson and orator and historian Dr. John Leslie Patton, Jr., who four decades ago taught the first black-history courses in Dallas public schools.

Emanu-El and Shearith Israel

Congregations Emanu-El and Shearith Israel organized two of the area's Jewish cemeteries. Founded in 1890 at 3430 Howell Street north of downtown (adjacent to Freedman's Cemetery and Greenwood Cemetery), Emanu-El is the older of the two. Among its neatly kept graves are those of early department store owners Adolph Harris and Philip and Alex Sanger (for whom the town of Sanger was named). There also are several dozen graves of early city residents who were moved here from Pioneer Cemetery when the convention center was expanded in late 1959. Other graves have names that reflect Russian, German and other European heritages. Many plots are delineated by concrete borders and are covered with gravel or "cribs" planted with ground cover.

Shearith Israel is along Dolphin Road south of Interstate 30 in East Dallas. It is not far from Grove Hill Cemetery and is adjacent to old Beeman Cemetery. Familiar names here include grocer Julius Schepps (his father, Nathan, founded Schepps Dairy; his cousins included philanthropist Julius, for whom Julius Schepps Freeway is named, and George, a Dallas sports entrepreneur). Here, as at Emanu-El, inscriptions are frequently in Hebrew.

© Leon Unruh

Calvary Hill and Hillcrest

Dallas' movers and shakers of recent years often may be found under simple stones in northside cemeteries. In the deep reaches of Calvary Hill Cemetery, a Catholic graveyard on Lombardy Lane, airline founder Thomas Braniff (who died in a private-plane crash in 1954) is just a short hop from hotelier Conrad Hilton, who once was married to Zsa Zsa Gabor.

At Hillcrest Memorial Park Cemetery on Northwest Highway, oilman Haroldson Lafayette Hunt, once one of the world's richest people, lies near 1950s tennis ace Maureen Connolly Brinker and former Texas governor and U.S. Senator W. Lee O'Daniel, who are not far from former Senator and Secretary of Defense nominee John Tower and actress Greer Garson Fogelson. Baseball great Mickey Mantle rests in the Hillcrest Mausoleum; use the North St. Mark Addition entrance.

Monument of Haroldson Lafayette Hunt, once one of the world's richest people

© Leon Unruh

Monument of Governor and U.S. Senator W. Lee O'Daniel

As with many cemeteries in Texas, Hillcrest began as a family cemetery and was expanded after the passage of a state law restricting the founding of cemeteries near cities, says Frances James, the preservationist. John Bailey, attorney for Greenwood Cemetery in Fort Worth, explains that a 1934 law, in the state Health and Safety Code, forbids the founding

Statuary at Hillcrest

of cemeteries within five miles of a city of more than 200,000 population. Smaller cities are allowed to have them closer to town.

Hillcrest was originally a Caruth family cemetery. That section is fenced off near Northwest Highway. (Restland Memorial Park, for another North Dallas example, originally was the Floyd family graveyard, Mrs. James says.) Hillcrest has such a parklike atmosphere that Dallas and Park Cities residents often bring their children to feed the koi in the pond near the entrance. It gives the impression of being the garden spot that Oakland Cemetery used to be.

Hillcrest's self-perception was put on the ropes not long ago when the Vehon family wanted to erect a statue of a nude man atop the family stone. "We decided our families weren't quite ready for that," Barbara Gross, Hillcrest's office manager, says with a laugh. The statue eventually was allowed, with discreet draping.

© Leon Unruh

Statue atop Vehon monument wears discreet draping.

Old Letot and Dallas City Cemetery

Old Letot Cemetery and Dallas City Cemetery are neighbors in North Dallas, just south of Walnut Hill Lane and west of Harry Hines Boulevard. Until it was swallowed up by Dallas in the booming 1960s, Letot was a farming village named after Clement Letot, a French immigrant who arrived in 1876 and bought 1,200 acres. (According to *The New Handbook of Texas*, he is also the only Dallas County resident to have fought in the Crimean War.) The cemetery, at 10700 Shady Trail, is up a small rise from the road and surrounded by a fence. Mr. Letot, who died in 1907, is buried two miles away in the Letot family cemetery attached to the north side of Calvary Hill Cemetery.

Dallas City Cemetery provides its inhabitants an almost secluded existence. It is reached by a gravel alley just north of an office park at 10606 Shady Trail. It was founded in the 1930s as a pauper's ground, Mrs. James says. With a few exceptions, graves are marked with a six-by-six-inch block of concrete that holds a small brass plate stamped with the deceased's name, birth date and death date.

Daniel and Wheatland

Sprinkled across Dallas and Tarrant counties are dozens of family and church cemeteries that hold pioneer residents. Dallas County alone has about 200 such cemeteries. Two of them still in use in the southwestern part of the county are Daniel and Wheatland. The Daniel family graveyard, close to Danieldale Road at Bolton Boone Drive in DeSoto, was set aside for descendants of the Reverend Ellison Daniel. Its earliest known burial was in 1857.

At 8000 Hampton Road in southwest Dallas, the Wheatland Cemetery holds members of the pioneering Nance and Penn ranching families, among many others. It is adjacent to the wonderful wooden Wheatland United Methodist Church, founded in 1847 and reputed to be the oldest Methodist Church west of the Trinity River.

Fish Trap

Fish Trap Cemetery, also known as Old French Colony Cemetery, is tucked into the northwest corner of Singleton Boulevard and Hampton Road, behind L. G. Pinkston High School on Fish Trap Road. The area was settled in 1855 by European immigrants who set up a short-lived Utopian settlement named La Réunion. The small cemetery, all that remains of the colony, is beautified by locust and oak trees and patches of irises. Surrounded by a tall chain-link fence, it has dozens of markers. Among the settlers buried here was naturalist Julien Reverchon (died 1905), for whom Dallas' Reverchon Park is named. The settlement's name was appropriated for a downtown arena and tower.

Western Heights and Crown Hill

Decades after they were shot to death in Louisiana, two of the Southwest's most famous lovers and outlaws are separated by seven miles. Officers of the law ambushed Clyde Barrow and Bonnie Parker in May 1934, ending their (some say his) run of bank robberies. Their bullet-riddled car and belongings have since been sold for thousands of dollars.

Clyde Barrow is buried in his family plot with brother Marvin "Buck" Barrow in Western Heights Cemetery, 1617 Fort Worth Avenue, in West Dallas, just a few miles up the road from where Clyde used to work at Trinity Portland Cement. The Barrows' plot is in the southwest corner beneath some shady crape myrtles.

Bonnie Parker first was buried in Fish Trap Cemetery. But after her headstone was stolen repeatedly, her grave was moved to Crown Hill Cem-

Bonnie Parker's grave at Crown Hill Cemetery

etery on Webb Chapel Road north of Dallas Love Field airport. People stumbling across Ms. Parker's flat headstone (west of the hedge near the entrance) never would guess her background.

The epitaph: "As the flowers are all made sweeter by the sunshine and the dew, so this old world is made brighter by the lives of folks like you."

A Monument Seller Brings Cemetery Landscape to Life

Leon Unruh

Dallas •

[*The Salesman's name appeared in the original newspaper story. Not long after the story appeared, however, he apparently closed his shop and left Dallas, followed by complaints about his business practices. Nevertheless, what he said about headstones was not disputed.*]

On a tour of Grove Hill Cemetery in East Dallas, The Salesman explains the heritage of headstones and other cemetery decorations. He knows his way around the business. As the owner of a Greenville Avenue memorial and monument company, he sells stones and markers directly to the public. Previously, he was a salesman for a private North Dallas cemetery.

© Leon Unruh

The Salesman stops at the Miller monument, a marble angel.

"You won't see a lot of statues with wings spread in this part of the country," he says. "She's a pretty thing. They just don't make them like that anymore."

But he is looking at discoloration, too. Marble produces a fine-looking statue, but it erodes relatively quickly and becomes discolored by lichens, bad air and water. Experts bleach marble with a peroxide mixture.

"Joe Blow don't need to be doing this," The Salesman says.

Statues nowadays, he says, usually are made in a mold from a mixture of marble fines (the "sawdust" of quarry work) and epoxy. Artisans in Italy still produce some hand-carved statues.

At first glance, Grove Hill has a lot of stumps among the gracious old trees. Those symbolically broken trees, however, are really a death benefit from the Woodmen of the World insurance company provided from 1890 until the 1920s, although some people continued to have them made long afterward. Ernie May, of the Omaha-based "fraternal benefit society," says that policyholders (who lived across the country but predominantly in the South) at first received the monuments as part of their ben-

A Woodmen of the World marker sits in the IOOF Cemetery in Ponca City, Oklahoma.

© Leon Unruh

efits, but that eventually a $100 rider was added to cover the cost. Today, The Salesman says, a custom stone such as that would cost about $25,000.

Mr. May, a senior staff writer in the Woodmen Communication Department, says the company hired local stonecutters to cut the stones to a certain plan, but the artisans often interpreted the instructions as they saw fit. The cost of the four- to five-foot-high stones and the growth of cemeteries that prohibited above-ground markers eventually brought an end to the company's practice. Despite their variations, however, most of the monuments carried the Latin phrase, "Dum Tacet Clamat" (Though Silent, He Speaks).

Many pink granite stones found in Dallas come from Marble Falls in Central Texas. Almost all gray stones come from Elberton, Georgia. Marble comes from Italy or a handful of U.S. sites. Granite is sawed from the mountain in sixteen-foot sections, The Salesman says, then cut into blanks that are polished and sent to sales offices, where the final touches are handled.

Artwork and lettering is laid out on a computer. An on-screen design—names and dates and a scene of Pa and his tractor, for example—is mechanically cut out of a rubber mat, making a template. The template is laid on the stone, and a sandblaster cuts away everything that is not protected by the mat. Raised lettering and artwork, seen occasionally, is more difficult to produce than recessed lettering because the artisans have to cut away everything that doesn't look like words or flowers. Because quarries want to cut stone efficiently, The Salesman says, there's a dearth of big pieces that could be used to make tall obelisks or heavy columns, even if a family could afford it. For mausoleums, he says, bring half a million dollars. Or two million dollars if you want a building as fancy as Jack Diamond's at Grove Hill. Mausoleums have their own special needs, he says. They must have air vents to prevent the accumulation of gases, and the bronze doors occasionally need to be stripped and refinished.

Often headstones are placed on the ground before the plot owners die. In those cases, cemeteries later hire sandblasters to visit a grave and carve death dates. Some souls faced the problem of having bought a stone bearing a death date beginning "19—." If they made it around the corner of the century, a carver will fill the "19" with a matching granite-epoxy mixture, then cut the four new numerals starting with "20—."

Jack Diamond's mausoleum at Grove Hill

City Fathers, Tycoons, Assassins: Fort Worth Neighbors Forever

Leon Unruh

One side of General Edward H. Tarrant's headstone in Pioneer's Rest goes on at length about his achievements in the War of 1812, the Texas War for Independence, the Texas Congress and the Indian wars.

The other side says it all: "This stone marks his final resting place. Tarrant County is his monument."

At one time a Republic of Texas congressman from Red River County, Mr. Tarrant resigned to fight Indians in 1837 and in 1839 was elected commander, equal to brigadier general, of a military organization known as the Fourth Brigade, according to *The New Handbook of Texas*. Although he and his wife eventually moved to a farm near Italy, Ellis County, in 1857 he helped raise attacks against the Indians again at Fort Belknap, near what is now Newcastle, Young County. While heading to Fort Belknap in 1858 he died and was buried near Weatherford; he was later reburied on his farm and reburied yet again in Pioneer's Rest about seventy years after his death.

Pioneer's Rest Cemetery, on Samuels Avenue northeast of downtown Fort Worth, was laid out near a tavern and a crossing point of the Trinity River used by drovers moving herds to the stockyards. The cemetery was started in 1850 to hold the graves of Sophie and Willis Arnold, the children of Major Ripley Arnold, the commander of Fort Worth, who founded a camp on the Trinity River in 1849 and named it after his recently deceased superior, General William Worth. Major Arnold, who is reported by *The New Handbook of Texas* to have been a truly unpleasant supervisor, was killed by a gunman (later acquitted) at Fort Graham in 1853. Pioneer's Rest holds Major Arnold's grave, marked by a stone—an actual boulder—and a plaque.

Near General Tarrant's and Major Arnold's stones stands a shaft on which the widow Byrne eulogizes her husband's death while fighting Indians in 1880 near Quitman in Wood County. Seventy-five Civil War veterans also are buried on the six-acre grounds.

Oakwood

Many of Fort Worth's early "glitterati" now rest at Oakwood Cemetery, on Grand Street north of the Trinity River from downtown. John Peter Smith, Winfield Scott, Samuel Burk Burnett and Charles Culberson (governor from 1895 to 1899) have graves or mausoleums on this pretty hillside. Mr. Smith, a Confederate colonel, came to be known as "the father of Fort Worth" because of his vast postwar business dealings and immense landholdings in Tarrant County; indeed, he donated the land for Oakwood and two other cemeteries, as well as for the hospital named after him. As a general officer in the 1840s invasion of Mexico, Mr. Scott once commanded Ripley Arnold and was a businessman after the Civil War. Mr. Burnett was a turn-of-the-century rancher-oilman who left six million dollars (back when that was real money) to Texas Christian University when he died in 1922. (Another early Fort Worth leader, Colonel Middleton Tate Johnson, was buried near his plantation in what is now Arlington. He may be visited at the Johnson Station Cemetery on Mayfield Road near Cooper Street.)

There is also a monument to Major Horace Carswell, a Medal of Honor winner for whom the former Air Force base was named. Look also for the eagle-decorated Fraternal Order of Eagles spire, and the grave of W. F. Whitlow, whose stone face juts out from his marker.

Greenwood

After the Civil War, U.S. soldiers came to collect the spoils of war. According to Julia Kathryn Garrett in her book *Fort Worth: A Frontier Triumph,* settler Richard Turner and his slave Uncle Ben buried his gold beneath an oak. The gold later helped the city survive the tight times of Reconstruction.

That tree stands at the entrance to Greenwood Cemetery on White Settlement Road. Nearby, on the Luse Wallenberg plot, a half-dressed woman lifts a monumental hurrah over a pot of coins. Laid to rest less

© Leon Unruh

ostentatiously on these lush riverside grounds are such worthies as Amon G. Carter, the newspaper publisher and civic booster; oilman Kenneth Davis; Mayor Henry Clay Meacham, for whom the city's airport was named; and Charles Tandy, the electronics manufacturer of Radio Shack fame.

Tandy mausoleum

Historical markers honor British pilots killed during training and Ormer Leslie Locklear, a barnstorming stunt pilot killed in 1920 while making his second movie in Hollywood.

Koslow monument

Rose Hill

Everyone knows his name, but no one will find it on a tombstone. Lee Harvey Oswald, who was shot dead for assassinating President Kennedy, lies along the western fence in this eastern Fort Worth cemetery. His deed was so notorious that his marker has been removed. Questions about whose remains the grave contained were settled in 1983 when the body was disinterred and examined. The experts said it was Oswald.

But Rose Hill is not about Oswald. A visitor around Memorial Day will stand in a sea of small American flags marking the graves of military personnel who died with honor. Elsewhere on the grounds are the ashes of Fort Worth's beloved KXAS-TV weatherman, Harold Taft, who died in 1991.

Texas' tiniest state historical park is the size of a boxing ring. It is a .006-acre burial plot in Acton Cemetery, six miles east of Granbury in Hood County. Davy Crockett's widow, Elizabeth, and their two children lie there.

The cemetery opened in 1855 as Comanche Peak; Mrs. Crockett died in 1860. Her tomb is surmounted by a heroic-size statue of the illustrious lady, added in 1911.

Jesse James Is Elusive in Death

Tom Simmons

Did the real Jesse James, notorious bad man of 125 years ago, lead three lives?

Cemetery buffs would have you think so. Else how could there be three "positive" burial grounds for Jesse, who died either in 1882, 1943 or 1951? Take your choice.

• The original grave is in Kearney, Missouri, twenty-five miles northeast of Kansas City and conveniently close to the spot where "Jesse" was assassinated April 3, 1882. A yellowed copy of the local newspaper gives all the details, and the area has a tidy tourist attraction as a result.

In Missouri, Jesse brings a steady stream of visitors—up to 20,000 a year—to see his grave in the City Cemetery to which it was moved in 1902. His old lodging nearby with memorabilia can be visited every day of the year for $4.50 or less. After other Jesses showed up, Kearney had a DNA test made a few years ago of the contents of the grave, and the scientists said there was only one chance in 308 that it could not be Jesse.

• Not so, say the folks in Granbury, Texas, the hustling tourist-minded seat of Hood County, seventy miles southwest of Dallas. Just go to the Granbury Cemetery, on the edge of downtown, and look at the simple white marker which says "Jesse Woodson James/Sept 5, 1847/Aug 15, 1951."

Granbury's story is that Jesse lived under various names in many places until he chose to come to Granbury when his end drew near. His kinfolks think he's there, and some of them show up from time to time. The Granbury Visitors Bureau says the question most asked of them—by far—is, where is Jesse James buried? Even visitors from overseas know about him and make the pilgrimage of a mile or so from the Visitors Center to see the site, visible from the road.

• The third claimant of ol' Jesse says his bones are in the Old Blevens Cemetery, near Marlin in Falls County. Kent Biffle wrote about it in *The Dallas Morning News* August 31, 1997, after he talked to Betty Luke of Liberty Hill in Williamson County. She says Jesse was her great-grandfather, and he was buried as James L. Courtney, October 31, 1846–April 14, 1943.

Ms. Luke has family photographs to substantiate her story. But it hasn't attracted the tourists. The Falls County Clerk has a death certificate to show, but that's about all.

There are the nominees. Will the real Jesse rise from the tomb and be recognized?

Granite Markers, Bricks, Crosses Mark Thurber's Multiethnic Graveyard

Tom Simmons

Thurber

Thurber, a busy coal mining town at the turn of the century with a population that reached more than 10,000, now lies just off Interstate 20 in Erath County, and you may not even be able to find it on a map. The current population is five—the O'Beirne family—which owns the Smokehouse Restaurant. The Texas & Pacific Coal Company picked out nine acres on a hilltop for a graveyard and burials began. The oldest tombstone remembers Eva Chapman, an infant who died in 1890. It served for more than a century, until 1993, when as private property it was no longer open to the casual sightseer. Access is generally restricted to descendants and relatives; a key can be borrowed from the restaurant.

During its busy years, the graveyard reflected the multiethnic community. Separate entrances led to Catholic, Protestant and African-American areas. The mine employed eighteen or twenty nationalities, many of them workers from Italy and Poland. There are at least 1,000 graves, more than half of them for infants and children, a reflection of epidemics of diphtheria, scarlet fever, whooping cough and malaria.

This history is gleaned from a marker put up by the Texas Historical Commission at the cemetery entrance on State Highway 108. A locked gate bears an outdated sign for the Texas and Southwestern Cattle Raisers Association.

Two hundred yards or so up a rough road is an unlocked gate marked "TP" for the coal company. Alongside it is a sign that the restoration was primarily due to the unfailing efforts of Leo S. Bielinski of Fort Worth and five associates. Bielinski's grandparents and other family members are there and he is planning for his own family to be there also.

In 1993 the Thurber Cemetery Monument was dedicated with 694 names on it: "Thou place of Repose is Known only to God but Thy Memory Remains with us," a bit ungrammatical, maybe. Bielinski and his associates come regularly to mow the grass. The monument was financed by bricks sold for $250 or $50, and bricks are still being sold by the Thurber Cemetery Association. The proceeds are used for maintenance. About the only burials now are kinspersons of the departed.

Strewed across the grassy, rocky hilltop are many simple white wooden crosses and rough stones (no names). A large wooden cross with pipes marks the graves of Barbara Lorenz, who died January 31, 1931, and John Lorenz, December 18, 1936. Scattered over the hill are iron fences; one plot surrounded by a brick wall contains a group of a half-dozen cedar trees, rare on the stark acreage.

Thurber Cemetery monument

Simple wooden crosses, this one surrounded by pipes, often serve as headstones.

Now on private property, the old Thurber Cemetery includes many graves from the 1800s—most unmarked.

Restoration other than Bielinski's, such as opening roads, were due to the landowners who own the restaurant. Kinfolks are welcome to borrow the key but others are regarded as a nuisance. Kids have played with headstones and done other mischief, as kids will.

LBJ Rests at His Beloved River Ranch

Leon Unruh

Johnson City

Lyndon Baines Johnson was a legendary host at his Hill Country ranch. The former teacher, congressman, senator, vice president and president often loaded dignitaries into a Cadillac and barreled through the pastures. Things are quieter now at the ranch, where the state's only deceased president (1908–1973) is buried in the family's spacious cemetery.

His substantial granite stone notes simply he was the nation's 36th president. His sixty-two-month presidency, highlighted by education and civil rights improvements and the Vietnam War, ended in 1969.

© Leon Unruh

LBJ's marker stands head and shoulders above those of his parents and other relatives.

LBJ's parents, Sam Ealy, Jr., and Rebekah Baines Johnson, siblings and some grandparents are there as well under the magnificent live oaks. His widow, Claudia Alta "Lady Bird" Johnson, lives in Austin.

The ranch is halfway between Johnson City and Fredericksburg in Gillespie County. To reach the ranch from Johnson City, drive west on U.S. Highway 290 to Park Road 1 near Hye. Turn right at the marked road to the ranch, cross the Pedernales River and turn left immediately on Park Road 49 at the Junction School. The cemetery is a short distance ahead near LBJ's reconstructed birthplace. The cemetery also can be reached through LBJ State Historical Park.

The graves lie within an iron fence, a short hedge and a stone fence. One plaque identifies the Johnson family graves, which march in a row across the cemetery, and another recites the first four lines from Thomas Gray's "Elegy Written in a Country Churchyard."

South of the Pedernales is the Gothic-style Trinity Lutheran Church, where the Johnsons sometimes worshiped. The church was built in 1928. There is a small cemetery west of the church.

Straight and Narrow Is the Path in Fredericksburg

Leon Unruh

Fredericksburg

You may never see a neater graveyard than Der Stadt Friedhof, The City Cemetery. Or a more severe cemetery. Or a more artistic one.

Fredericksburg, an arts-and-crafts boom town in the Hill Country, was laid out in 1846 by German noblemen, the Adelsverein, who were planting colonies in Texas. True to their pan-Germanic heritage, they liked things to line up squarely, from the hewn-stone street curbs in town to the rows in the cemetery.

"We were almost neurotic about structure," says Glen Treibs, a high-school history teacher for thirty years who has retired to his ranch and two bed-and-breakfasts. Mr. Treibs is recognized locally as an expert on the twenty-seven-acre cemetery, which lies along a creek downstream from town. At age fifty-two, he is a fifth-generation Texan who pronounces

Hier ruht in Gott (Here rests in God)

84

"Luckenbach" with a long -ch and uses "we" in speaking about the colonists.

"My eight families moved here, and we've never lived anywhere else in the Western Hemisphere," he says.

The 5,000 graves in Der Stadt Friedhof are lined up neatly, with little plant life to soften the appearance. Although many nineteenth-century graves have wrought-iron fences, the newer ones have concrete curbs. In some parts of the cemetery, entire rows of graves are covered with concrete and gravel.

"It's so much better for maintenance and so much more meticulous," Mr. Treibs says. "We do the whole row; we have a temporary topping on it" that is removed when a grave is to be opened.

Although Der Stadt Friedhof is open to anyone's family, Mr. Treibs acknowledges that old-time Gillespie County families may be more likely to buy plots here. Indeed, many stones have German inscriptions: for example, "Hier ruht in Gott" (Here rests in God). Unlike in cemeteries where families bought large plots, graves here tend to march down the row. Everyone who died in, say, 1932, was buried in order of death. "Babyland" graves are handled the same way.

"We just said people would be buried as they fell," Mr. Treibs says.

Exceptions would be the mass graves and those belonging to black Americans who died in the 1800s. Following American tradition, the few black residents were buried in their own walled section toward the back of the cemetery. In Fredericksburg's first years, a cholera epidemic killed dozens, who were buried in mass graves in Der Stadt Friedhof.

To find the cemetery from U.S. Highway 290, turn north at Washington, at the Admiral Nimitz Museum and Historical Center, and east at Schubert.

Der Stadt Friedhof used to have a big tree in the middle of the cemetery, but it is dead now. Its limbs are cut back to the tall trunk, echoing symbolically the Woodmen of the World's stumplike stones. Trees are not welcome among the graves, Mr. Treibs says, although a few trees have been planted recently where their roots are not likely to cause trouble. Some of the older, fenced plots have nearly been consumed by trees or prickly pears. One of the cemetery's mysteries, Mr. Treibs says, concerns early gravestones. The earliest ones faced west, but the newer ones face east. What inspired the change?

"We have no clue," he says. "I even asked Germans when I was over in Germany."

The cemetery was founded in 1846 when the town was. The oldest legible grave marker, Mr. Treibs says, is from 1849. Eroded badly now, it was carved in limestone from Cross Mountain just north of town. Later stones were created from Bear Mountain red granite, taken from a quarry near Enchanted Rock. There also are markers of gray granite. As strait-laced as the old Germans may have been, they topped the dearly departed off with loads of symbolism. A Civil War veteran has a cannon and cannonballs. Some stones sport carvings of anchors (as in, Jesus is a Christian's anchor), or gates of heaven, or stars or hearts or porcelain portraits.

The cemetery, Mr. Treibs says, is "our biggest art museum."

Famed Austin artist Elisabet Ney sculpted a cherub on commission for a woman's grave. Thieves have taken several little angels from children's graves, an act Mr. Treibs attributes to the current "rage over angels." Visitors should not miss the old section's ironwork and metal decorations. Historian Terry Jordan, in his *Texas Graveyards: A Cultural Legacy*, lauds the German graveyards of Gillespie County for their artwork, which ranges from traditional hex stars to sheet-metal crosses and "witch's feet."

Elizabet Ney cherub at Der Stadt Friedhof

Trees are not welcome at Der Stadt Friedhof.

Der Stadt Friedhof's dead, Mr. Treibs says, include members of Lyndon Baines Johnson's extended family; a man found in a field with a dozen arrows in him whose inscription says "murdered by Indians"; and an unknown girl found in Gillespie County in the 1920s. Boy Scouts took care of her funeral. Fredericksburg's most famous native, Fleet Admiral Chester Nimitz, is remembered in town for his World War II career. His birthplace and a state historical park and museum downtown carry his name. The admiral, however, retired on the West Coast and is buried in San Bruno, California.

The city has more cemeteries of note: St. Mary's, a Catholic graveyard west of town, and Greenwood, a contemporary park with trees and grass north of town. Mr. Treibs points out that Der Stadt Friedhof has been run almost since the start by an association of Lutheran churches. All in all, things have not changed much over the years.

"If we like something," he says, "we like it the way it was."

The Salt of the Earth Are Interred in Austin

Bob Bersano

Austin

On December 26, 1851, General Edward Burleson died in Austin after a distinguished career as a soldier and statesman. He was a hero of thirty battles, senior colonel for Stephen F. Austin, Battle of San Jacinto veteran, vice president of the Republic of Texas and a state senator. Where would such a distinguished individual be buried? Declaring General Burleson "one of the links to the great and glorious past of the Republic of Texas," his fellow senators formed a committee to plan his funeral and burial services. The senators wished to establish a "state burying ground" for prominent citizens, and on December 28, 1851, General Burleson was buried on the east Austin site that eventually became the Texas State Cemetery, a favorite stopping place for families and history buffs.

Notables buried here include former governors James E. "Pa" Ferguson, Miriam A. "Ma" Ferguson, Dan Moody, Allan Shivers, and John Connally, as well as Texas writers J. Frank Dobie, Walter Prescott Webb and Fred Gibson (who penned *Old Yeller*). Educator and former U.S. Representative

Stephen F. Austin monument designed by Pompeo Coppini

Barbara Jordan was buried here in a moving service in 1996.

photo courtesy Texas State Cemetery

"It's one of my favorite places for a nostalgic look back in time," says native Texan Lyall Davis of Dallas. "I see beautiful and interesting monuments and statues plus attractive and well-kept grounds."

Texas State Cemetery entrance

The idea for a state resting place quickly caught on. One week after General Burleson's death, the Texas State Legislature voted to move the remains of Stephen F. Austin from Brazoria County to Austin. Doing so, the resolution said, would honor "the memory of an individual who was the instrument in the hands of a wise Providence in laying the foundation of their prosperity and but for whose enterprise and fortitude this fertile and beautiful land would now and perhaps for ages to come have been a wild waste uninhabited by civilized man."

So Texas joined the ranks of states that envisioned a cemetery/museum, to provide a final resting place for notable citizens. Nevertheless, a dispute with Austin's family prevented the famed Texan's reburial until 1911.

The thousands of headstones, markers and monuments in the cemetery today are a stark contrast to the early years. The cemetery got off to a slow start, with just six burials in the ten years following the state's purchase of the property in 1854. Among them

photo courtesy Texas State Cemetery

were Abner S. Lipscomb, associate justice, and John Hemphill, chief of the Texas Supreme Court; General Benjamin McCulloch, San Jacinto and Mexican War veteran; and General William R. Scurry, Mexican War veteran and Civil War casualty.

In 1866, with Austin occupied by Federal troops, the legislature set aside a section of the cemetery for burial of U.S. soldiers who died while on duty in the Texas capital. Those bodies were later removed and reburied at the U.S. National Cemetery in San Antonio. Burials increased with the deaths of Civil War veterans. In 1886, a home for disabled and indigent Confederate veterans was opened in Austin, and as the men died, they were buried at the Texas State Cemetery beneath 2,300 white-marble headstones.

Governor O. B. Colquitt brought extensive improvements to the grounds in the early twentieth century, including the installation of many of the cemetery's most striking sculptures and monuments. In 1906, Austin sculptor Elisabet Ney unveiled a reclining marble figure she designed for the grave of Albert Sidney Johnston, Confederate general who fell at the battle of Shiloh. It is covered by a Gothic metal structure that is one of the cemetery's most distinctive features.

Grave of Albert Sidney Johnston

Italian-born Pompeo Coppini designed a bronze statue for Austin's grave, as well as a statue of Joanna Troutman, who designed an early Texas Lone Star flag. Enrico Cerracchio, another Italian-born sculptor, designed a bronze bust for Battle of San Jacinto hero General John A. Wharton. By 1935, seventy-six individuals had been moved from their original burial sites to Austin, including former governors James Pinckney Henderson and Peter Hanborough Bell, former lieutenant governor John A. Greer, and a group of Republic of Texas veterans and signers of the Texas Declaration of Independence.

Over the decades that followed, the cemetery fell into neglect. Faced with crumbling gravestones, decaying roads and overgrown trees on the eighteen-acre site, Lieutenant Governor Bob Bullock, in 1994, spurred state agencies to develop a master plan to restore the graveyard to incorporate a historical perspective and pride to the setting.

Three years later, the Texas State Cemetery was rededicated. It now features a new visitor center constructed of hand-worked limestone, an observation hill for a view of the cemetery and its surroundings, interpretive paths leading visitors through the grounds and a memorial pond that enhances a sense of tranquility.

A new ceremonial entrance is flanked by a massive granite mausoleum. On the cemetery's south side, a striking plaza surrounded by giant stone tablets relates significant moments in history and honors people who made important contributions to the state.

"The design creates a much greater opportunity for contemplation," says Andrew Sansom, executive director of the Texas Parks and Wildlife Department.

Those interred are here because each contributed an important thread to Texas history. Not all of them are well-known, but each has a story to tell. Among the near-forgotten are:

• Robert (Three-Legged Willie) Williamson, who wore a wooden leg attached to his knee in the Battle of San Jacinto; he was the first judge of the district court in the Republic of Texas and later served in Congress.

• James Austin Sylvester, who carried a flag in the Battle of San Jacinto that is now displayed in the State Capitol behind the speaker's rostrum.

• Gideon Lincecum, a self-educated physician, naturalist and philosopher, who worked with scientists such as Charles Darwin and who recorded the legends and traditions of the Choctaw Indians.

• Jacob Raphael de Cordova, a Jewish businessman who supplied Texas with staples during the revolution, and who produced the first map of the state. Oddly, the stone marking his grave is adorned with a cross.

At the south end of the cemetery, the Plaza de Los Recuerdos is a place to remember all Texans who have made contributions to the state. In the plaza's center is a huge limestone rock representing a Hill Country landscape. A computerized fountain creates four small lakes, which represent rainfall during the four seasons.

"This area is a place to reflect and to be reminded of Texas history," says Laura David of the Texas Parks and Wildlife Department.

The cemetery is an impressive place to learn about Texas history through the stories of people who lived it.

"It's the place where a broader group of Texans, including those who have been left out and new Texans, can learn about Texas history and take pride in it," Mr. Sansom says.

The Texas State Cemetery, four blocks east of downtown, is bounded by East 7th Street on the south, East 11th Street on the north, Navasota Street on the west and Comal Street on the east. There is limited parking in front of the visitor center on Navasota Street.

The cemetery and visitor center are open Monday through Friday, 8 A.M. to 5 P.M., and the grounds are open on weekends. For more information about the cemetery, or to inquire about arranging group field trips, call (512) 463-0605.

Graveyard Is All That Remains of Dobyville

Leon Unruh

Dobyville

It is no longer even a wide spot in the road. In the late 1800s, however, the northern Burnet County hamlet of Dobyville had dozens of residents. It had a post office off and on between 1874 and 1900, and it boasted a school, a cotton gin and grist and syrup mills. Civilization had arrived, but life still bordered on the brutish in these hills wrested from the Comanches.

The New Handbook of Texas reports that in the first decades of the 1900s, Dobyville's annual spring fling was a day of picnicking and rabbit drives, in which hundreds of the pests were encircled and pushed inward to be slaughtered. Hard times and hard limestone—the town's name was derived from the "adobe" rock underlying the area—eventually wore the people out. A few houses were left in the 1940s; now there's not even a ghost town here amid the mesquite trees.

But the cemetery is still in use. As with so many other little graveyards across Texas, it provides a singular glimpse into a lost town's history. Jacob and Adeline Wolf, Tennessee immigrants who pioneered in the 1850s and were among the founders of Burnet County, are buried under ornate white markers inside a stone fence. Jacob's marker is incorporated into the stone-and-mortar fence surrounding their plot. Two of their sons became sheriffs, one in Burnet County, the other in neighboring Lampasas County.

Jacob Wolf's marker is incorporated into the fence.

Another old Texas name found under the junipers is O'Hair. Nearby O'Hair's Hill, now defunct, had a post office in the 1870s. Several graves follow the Southern tradition of being outlined with rocks and white-rock crosses decorate a few. The earliest known grave, according to a state historical marker, belongs to Mary Standefer (1833–1857). There are about 230 marked graves, as well as sixty to seventy unmarked graves thought to be those of infants.

Travelers on U.S. Highway 281 will speed past the Dobyville cemetery unless they keep an eye open near the junction with County Road 103, about eleven miles north of Burnet.

Toad Tale Had Hoppy Ending

Jean Simmons

Eastland

He lies in state in the Eastland County Courthouse, resting on purple velvet and white satin. Jerry Don Reeves, "his personal maid," is polishing the glass that protects him. A tour bus is on its way, so clear visibility is important. For here lies Eastland's most famous corpse: Old Rip, a horned toad.

The oft-told story of Old Rip bears repeating. In 1897, when the cornerstone of the new courthouse was dedicated, Justice of the Peace Earnest Wood, a member of the band, noticed that his son Will was playing with a toad. Let's put him in the cornerstone, he decided. There the toad lived peacefully buried until February 18, 1928, when the courthouse was demolished to make way for a new one.

Three thousand people were on hand, anxious to watch the opening of the cornerstone. Judge E. S. Pritchard removed the Bible and other objects, and at the bottom was the toad. Eugene Day, an oil man, thrust his hand into the cavity and lifted up the dust-covered creature. He handed it to Frank S. Singleton, pastor of the First United Methodist Church, who passed it on to Judge Pritchard, who in turn held it up by the tail for all to see.

Suddenly Old Rip awoke from his thirty-one-year-sleep. No wonder he is called Rip, after Washington Irving's Rip Van Winkle. In the months that followed, he was exhibited in various parts of the United States, including a visit to President Coolidge in Washington, until he died of pneumonia on January 19, 1929.

A biologist explained how Rip might have survived in the cornerstone: Horned toads, as with many lizards, can slow their metabolism in cool weather, and a crack might have allowed ants to enter, providing food. After being embalmed, Rip was given a place of honor just inside the main courthouse entrance. A conventional granite marker outside the building calls attention to what lies just on the other side of an above window: a glass box containing the long-dead toad. A missing leg has been attributed to the late Governor John Connally, who on a whistle-stop tour in 1962 either picked up the frog while there or took him off to Cisco, where he was retrieved.

County Judge Scott Bailey is Old Rip's guardian angel, keeper of the key to his box. The toad is always referred to as "he," but who really knows? Judge Bailey isn't saying.

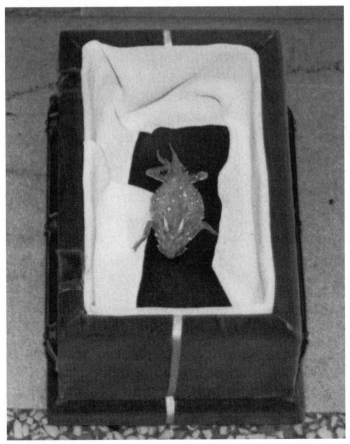

Old Rip

With Soldiers Gone, Only Civilians Rest at Old Fort Stockton

Bryan Woolley

• Fort Stockton

The Old Fort Cemetery used to be the burial ground for soldiers stationed at Fort Stockton and for civilians who died in the tiny town near the fort. After the Army abandoned the fort in 1886, the military dead were moved to San Antonio, but the civilians remain. About two dozen tombstones are still in the little sunbaked plot, which is now surrounded by industrial buildings and equipment yards. Most of the stones have fallen over or been broken. The historical marker at the cemetery gate states: "This cemetery testifies to the hardships of frontier life. No headstone was erected for a person over 40."

Not true. Among the remaining residents of the Old Fort Cemetery are Barney K. Riggs (1856–1902), Robert B. Neighbors (1856–1904) and Hermann Koehler (1849–1894).

The tombstone of A. J. Royal (1855–1894), tells the world he was "Assassinated." Mr. Royal's son, Andrew Roy Royal, shares his father's plot. He was not quite two years old when he died. Equally touching is the grave of seventeen-year-old Inez Powers (1883–1901). Her inscription reads: "A friend of the friendless, a help to the helpless. In her mercy and truth met together."

(above)
Old Fort
Cemetery
(left)
Inez Powers'
monument

Pioneer Graveyard Recalls Hard Times in Fort Davis

Bryan Woolley

• Fort Davis

For many years, this abandoned graveyard was just part of a fenced-in pasture on the outskirts of Fort Davis, and few people knew of it. Now there's a gate and a historical marker at its entrance and a sidewalk leading to it. Among those buried in Pioneer Cemetery are Diedrick Dutchover (1820–1904) and his wife Refugio (1842–1908, also known as Cora), two of the first European settlers of the Davis Mountains.

Mr. Dutchover's name originally was Anton Diedrick. Shortly after his arrival in America from

The Dutchover graves

Belgium, he enlisted in the Army to serve in the Mexican War. The recruiting sergeant couldn't understand his poor English, so he enlisted him as "Dutch-All-Over." The young immigrant shortened the name to Dutchover and kept it.

Mr. Dutchover came to Fort Davis with the Army during the Indian Wars and at various times made his living as a scout, stagecoach driver and rancher. He and his wife, an immigrant from Spain, had many children. Their descendants are scattered all over the Southwest.

Not far from the Dutchover graves, which are surrounded by a rusty iron fence, is the unmarked burial place of Jube and Arthur Frier, two young horse thieves who on September 28, 1896, were killed by Texas Rangers. They were buried with their boots on in a common grave, the only boot-hill grave in Jeff Davis County.

When they killed him, the Rangers didn't know Arthur Frier's first name, so a board with "J Frier" carved into it served as the marker for both brothers. The board decayed and, in about 1950, fell down. It is now displayed in the Overland Trail Museum in Fort Davis.

A gravestone carved from pink sandstone from Dolores Mountain

Many of the gravestones in the little cemetery were carved by grieving family members from the soft pink sandstone found on nearby Dolores Mountain. Most of the inscriptions are in Spanish. Other graves are marked with ordinary field stones with no names or dates on them. Some are just piles of rocks.

Dolores Mountain was named for Dolores Doporto, the heroine of a romantic and tragic story: Her fiance was a young shepherd who tended his sheep west of town. On the eve of their wedding, Dolores climbed a mountain near her home and lighted a fire, a beacon of love for her sweetheart. But her lover didn't show up for the wedding. A search party later found his body. He had been killed by Indians. Dolores' grief drove her insane. Until her death thirty years later, she kept climbing the mountain at night and lighting fires, hoping in vain her lover would reply.

The historical marker says Dolores is buried in the cemetery at the foot of her mountain. But if she is, nobody knows where.

A small pile of dirt in the cemetery tells another sad tale. It once was an above-ground adobe tomb. It contained the bodies of seven children of the Bentley family, all of whom died within two weeks during an 1891 diphtheria epidemic.

Emily Legend Ends at an Empty Grave

Bryan Woolley

• Fort Davis

For many years, every tourist who came to Fort Davis heard the wonderful story of Indian Emily. It goes like this:

After a harrowing fight between cavalrymen from the fort and a band of Apaches, the victorious soldiers found a young American Indian girl abandoned on the battlefield. They carried her back to Fort Davis with them. The colonel's wife pitied the child, took her into her home and named her Emily. As she grew, Emily became the lady's companion and servant.

Sometime during her teen years, Emily fell in love with a lieutenant at the post named Tom Easton. Of course, she never revealed her feelings to the young man, so how could he know? He fell in love with the post's new schoolmarm and married her. Heartbroken, Emily sneaked away and rejoined the Apaches in the mountains. Then one night Emily overheard the chiefs plotting an attack on the fort. Fearing they might kill her beloved, Emily crept into the darkness and returned to Fort Davis to warn Tom. As she approached the post, a sentry spotted her and shouted, "Halt!"

Emily didn't. The sentry fired, wounding her mortally. But before she died, she gasped her warning to Lieutenant Easton. When the Apaches attacked, the soldiers were ready for them. The grateful cavalrymen buried Emily in their post cemetery.

After the Army abandoned Fort Davis in 1891, the soldiers buried there were moved to the national cemetery in San Antonio. But Emily was left behind in her unmarked grave under a pile of rocks. In 1936, the State of Texas erected a granite monument over Emily's grave, commemorating her brave sacrifice. Its inscription reads: "Here lies Indian Em'ly, an Apache girl whose love for a young officer induced her to give warning of an Indian attack. Mistaken for an enemy, she was shot by a sentry, but saved the garrison from massacre."

Local historian Barry Scobee included Emily's story in his book, *Old Fort Davis*, and in brochures promoting Fort Davis as a

Monument for Indian Emily was erected by the State of Texas.

tourist destination. Other writers picked it up and sold several versions of it to the Western pulp magazines. Over the years, many residents and visitors drove the dirt road to her grave to pay their respects.

In the 1960s, the federal government took over the old adobe post, restored many of its ruins and named it a national historic site. Delving into old military archives, federal historians made some surprising discoveries: There was no record that Fort Davis soldiers ever rescued an Indian girl or that the wife of any colonel who commanded Fort Davis ever befriended one; no lieutenant or any other soldier named Tom Easton ever served there; neither the Apaches nor any other tribe ever attacked the post. Nobody is buried in Indian Emily's grave.

"Barry Scobee believed the story was true," says Park Ranger Allan Morris. "His version was based on several oral-history versions that had been passed down in the town. He didn't have the military records and other factual sources that would have allowed him to conclude that Indian Emily couldn't have been anything but legend."

The feds hauled away the rocks that covered the sacred spot and closed the road to the site. Years later, they removed Emily's monument to the museum collection at Fort Davis National Historic Site.

Legendary El Paso Never Buried Its Wild West Heritage

Bryan Woolley

Out in the West Texas town of El Paso they've been burying in Concordia Cemetery since the 1850s. In those days, the graveyard was three miles from a tiny adobe village on the north bank of the Rio Grande. Now it's only a couple of blocks from Interstate 10, El Paso's east-west expressway, and surrounded by the state's fourth-largest city. Even whizzing by on the highway overpass, you do a double take when you glimpse Concordia, because it looks so much like what it is: a desolate frontier graveyard.

Concordia Cemetery

And as you enter the cemetery gate and see tumbleweeds blowing across the barren brown land and cactuses and the few dusty cedars standing among the stark, sun-hot tombstones, you almost can hear that eerie whistle of death that accompanies the Man With No Name in those early Clint Eastwood Westerns.

But El Paso isn't Hollywood. It's as down-to-earth, no-nonsense and real as a city can be. The dangerous border village from which it grew was real, too. Its deadly wildness made such legendary hard-case towns as Tombstone, Dodge City and Deadwood seem orderly and serene by comparison.

Many of the early graves were never marked and, because of nonchalant or nonexistent record-keeping, their locations now are unknown. Others had wooden markers that weather erased or destroyed, and time and vandals have defaced many tombstones. Even the grave of Concordia's best-known resident, notorious man-killer John Wesley Hardin, shot to death in 1895, was not marked until 1965, when a group of citizens got together and bought him a small stone. Mr. Hardin was the baddest of Western bad men, tougher, meaner and deadlier than Jesse James, Wild Bill Hickok, Billy the Kid, Wyatt Earp or any other frontier gunman on either side of the law. Leon Metz, who wrote his biography, says he killed between twenty and fifty men, "probably closer to fifty," but always claimed he never killed anyone who didn't need killing. Hardin's definition of "need," though, probably could have used some tinkering. One man died just for snoring in Mr. Hardin's presence.

But on a hot August night while Mr. Hardin was drinking and rolling dice at the Acme Saloon, El Paso Constable John Selman walked in, shot him in the back of the head and pumped two more slugs into him as he lay dead. The killing had nothing to do with Constable Selman's law-enforcement duties. It was a personal matter.

Less than a year later, another sometime lawman named George Scarborough shot Constable Selman dead outside the Wigwam Saloon, only a couple of blocks from where Mr. Selman had killed Mr. Hardin. Constable Selman was buried in Concordia, too, but nobody bothered to mark his grave. Now nobody knows where it is. Mr. Metz thinks it may be somewhere near Mr. Hardin's because that neighborhood of the cemetery was a sort of boot hill.

Indeed, just two graves from Mr. Hardin's, an outlaw named Martin M'Rose is buried. A few months before his own death, Mr. Hardin had hired Mr. Scarborough and two other law officers to murder Mr. M'Rose, whose wife, Beulah, was Mr. Hardin's mistress. Mrs. M'Rose paid Mr. Hardin's funeral expenses.

So it went in old El Paso.

Although the city does almost nothing to promote its wild-West past as a tourist attraction, hundreds of visitors manage to find their way to Mr. Hardin every year. Many leave plastic flowers, decks of cards, empty whiskey bottles and toy six-shooters on the grave, even letters they've written to the killer. In 1997, a group of citizens from Gonzales County— including some Hardin descendants—decided a John Wesley Hardin grave would be a nice attraction for their own region. They made a trip to El Paso to dig him up and carry him back to the place where he once had made his home.

When they arrived at Concordia, a posse of El Paso history buffs, news media and police met them at the grave. No shots were fired, but the Gonzales County people went away without Mr. Hardin. To forestall other such attempts, El Paso has since poured about three inches of concrete over the grave and re-covered it with dirt.

In other parts of Concordia, various ethnic, religious and fraternal groups—Catholics, Protestants, Jews, African-Americans, Masons, Oddfellows—have claimed their own sections. Only a few steps from Mr. Hardin's grave is the Chinese Cemetery, which is walled off from the rest of Concordia because the people

The Chinese Cemetery

buried there were considered heathens and couldn't be lowered into holy ground. Many buried under the flat concrete slabs, inscribed in Chinese characters, were descendants of laborers who helped build the railroads through El Paso in the nineteenth century. Others came to El Paso as refugees from across the Rio Grande during the Mexican Revolution of 1910–20.

Jake Erlich, who was billed "the tallest man in the world" when he traveled with the Barnum & Bailey Circus, is buried in his family's plot in the Jewish section. Mr. Erlich is said to have been 8-foot-7. Barnum & Bailey exhibited him alongside Tom Thumb, "the smallest man in the world."

Near the entrance to the Masonic section is a large granite vault that used to be the tomb of two prominent figures of the Mexican Revolution. One, Pascual Orozco, eventually was returned to his homeland and given the funeral of a national hero. The other, Victoriano Huerta, was reviled as a traitor to the revolution and moved to an inconspicuous grave in another El Paso cemetery.

In the beginning of the revolution, General Huerta was the highest military confidant of Mexico's revolutionary president, Francisco Madero, the guiding spirit of the 1910–20 revolution in its early stages. But in 1913, he engineered the assassination of President Madero and

The Masonic vault, once the tomb of two Mexican revolution leaders, is now a tool shed.

seized control of the government. Pancho Villa, Venustiano Carranza and other revolutionary leaders then rebelled against General Huerta and marched on Mexico City, eventually driving the dictator into exile in Spain.

In 1914, after General Carranza became president, another disenchanted revolutionary, General Orozco, persuaded General Huerta to return to North

America and lead another revolt against the government. But a few months later, U.S. troops arrested the pair at the tiny town of Newman, Texas, north of El Paso, where they were getting off a train and about to try to sneak into Mexico. They were placed under house arrest in El Paso. General Orozco jumped bond and was killed near Sierra Blanca, Texas, by Texas Rangers and others, supposedly for resisting arrest. His body was placed in the borrowed tomb at Concordia.

A few months later, General Huerta, a heavy drinker, died of cirrhosis of the liver. He joined General Orozco in the tomb. In the 1930s the Mexican government declared General Orozco a hero of the revolution and returned his body to his hometown for burial. But Mexico didn't want the villainous General Huerta. He remained in the tomb until his family decided to move him to nearby Evergreen Cemetery in 1936, where he still lies.

Concordia caretakers now use the warriors' old tomb as a tool shed.

Only Huerta's name was on the tombstone his family put over his grave when he was moved to Evergreen Cemetery. Even that eventually became worn and dim. Years later, two relatives from Mexico City gave him a new monument. Though still modest, it gives the dates of his birth and death and identifies him as a general and a president of Mexico.

Not far from General Huerta lies Albert B. Fall (1861–1944), one of New Mexico's first U.S. senators and Secretary of the Interior in President Warren G. Harding's administration. He was a key figure in the Teapot Dome scandal.

Government scandals in those days weren't as racy as our modern ones. Teapot Dome involved federal oil leases. The U.S. Senate accused Secretary Fall of accepting $300,000 in bribes from two millionaires, and in return giving them oil leases on federal lands without competitive bidding. Secretary Fall insisted the money was loans, not bribes, but in 1929 he was convicted of conspiracy and bribery and served nine months of a one-year prison term. He then moved to El Paso and spent the rest of his days trying to clear his name.

A couple of gunfighters who died with their boots on (El Paso had plenty of them) also are buried in Evergreen. Manen Clements, a cousin of John Wesley Hardin, was shot to death in the Coney Island Saloon in 1908. Witnesses said they didn't see a thing. Mr. Clements' grave is marked with a Woodmen of the World tombstone.

Bass Outlaw was shot to death in the back yard of Tillie Howard's whorehouse by John Selman, who later also killed John Wesley Hardin. Mr. Outlaw's grave is unmarked, but it can be located with the help of the cemetery's friendly staff.

See also p. 195 for National Cemeteries in Texas.

New Mexico

Santa Fe Graves Remember Wars of Soldiers and the Soul

Bryan Woolley

Santa Fe

In 1987, a man excavating the foundation for his new house near Glorieta, New Mexico, uncovered a mass grave containing the remains of thirty-one Confederate soldiers. They were members of the Texas Mounted Volunteers who were killed in the Battle of Glorieta Pass on March 28, 1862. The Texans, led by General Henry Sibley, had invaded the Territory of New Mexico hoping to capture Santa Fe and several U.S. forts. They planned to establish a Confederate foothold in the West and eventually seize control of the gold fields of Colorado and California.

They defeated Union forces in the Battle of Valverde and occupied Santa Fe. They also won the later Glorieta fight, but Confederate losses were heavy, and Union soldiers destroyed General Sibley's supply train. He was forced to abandon Santa Fe and retreat to Texas. The Civil War in New Mexico was over. However, when the home builder uncovered the remains of the fallen soldiers, another Texas-New Mexico battle ensued. Texas Governor Bill Clements wanted the Texans' remains returned for burial in the State Cemetery at Austin, but New Mexico refused to give them up.

Eventually Confederate Major John Shropshire, twenty-eight when he died, was identified by his officer's boots and spurs and two finely wrought rings he wore. He was reburied in 1990 beside his parents in Kentucky. Private J. S. Cotton, twenty, also was identified through his ring, which bore his name. And Private Ebineezer "Abe" Hanna, at seventeen the youngest of the dead soldiers, was identified by a pouchful of pencils that lay beside his body. He had been the company scribe. In 1993, Private Cotton and Private Hanna were buried in the Santa Fe National Cemetery, and tombstones were erected over them. The twenty-eight soldiers who still were unidentified were interred in another mass

Pvt. Ebineezer Hanna died at Glorieta Pass.

grave, this one marked by a small monument bearing a bronze plaque.

Although the Texans are not in their native soil, they lie in a beautiful place. The site of the Santa Fe National Cemetery, which lies on a hillside facing the west, brings a lump to the throat of any who sees it, especially when its thousands of tombstones are aglow in a New Mexico sunset. And near the Texans is a unique monument that tells another sad story. It is the grave of Private Dennis O'Leary, a lonely and sickly soldier who died at Fort Wingate, New Mexico, in 1901.

The story is that Private O'Leary was a desperately unhappy young man who did not mix well with his fellow soldiers. One day he disappeared from Fort Wingate and was reported AWOL. Several weeks later, he showed up again without an explanation for his absence. He was court-martialed and sentenced to a stay in the guardhouse, which he served without complaint. But on April 1, 1901, Private O'Leary shot himself to death. He left a note saying he had left a "memento" in the mountains and giving directions to it. A troop of soldiers with a buckboard went into the mountains to seek it. There they found a large tombstone carved out of sandstone. It was the statue of an almost-life-size soldier, wearing boots and cartridge belt, reclining against the trunk of a tree. Behind the trunk was the inscription: "Dennis O'Leary Pvt., Co. 1, 23 Infty, died Apr. 1, 1901, age 23 yrs. & 9 mo." During his weeks away from Fort Wingate, Private O'Leary had carved his own tombstone and inscribed the date of his death.

The tombstone carved by Pvt. O'Leary while AWOL

A Fugitive in Life, Billy's Behind Bars

Bryan Woolley

Fort Sumner

The law had no luck keeping Billy the Kid locked up when he was alive, but he is securely behind bars now. His grave is enclosed in a large steel cage. Chains and padlocks secure the cage door. His footstone is embedded in concrete and held down by heavy steel straps. Vandals made all this necessary. They kept chipping away pieces of the large tombstone that the Kid shares with two buddies, fellow outlaws Tom O'Folliard and Charlie Bowdrie. And thieves twice have lifted the Kid's smaller footstone and carried it away. It was stolen in 1950 and recovered twenty-six years later in Granbury, Texas; it was stolen again in 1981 and recovered a few days later in Huntington Beach, California.

All three outlaws who lie in the cage were dispatched to eternity by Pat Garrett, intrepid sheriff of Lincoln County, New Mexico. Sheriff Garrett killed Mr. O'Folliard and Mr. Bowdrie in separate shootouts during a manhunt in December 1880. He shot down their leader, Billy the Kid, seven months later in the bedroom of Fort Sumner rancher Pete Maxwell.

Billy the Kid's tombstone

118

Monument above the graves of the three outlaw pals

Billy the Kid, whose birth name was Henry McCarty, (alias William Antrim, alias William Bonney, the name on his footstone) is America's most famous—and probably most romantic—desperado. He made his name as a gunfighter during the late 1870s in the infamous Lincoln County War, a deadly contest between two factions for economic and political power in the remote New Mexican mountains. He was just a teenager at the time, hence his name. When the war ended with almost everybody dead, the Kid turned to gambling and cattle rustling for his livelihood, and he was a skillful man killer.

He apparently was a friendly, likeable young man, fun to be around, popular with women and loyal to his friends. Legend portrays him as a sort of Western Robin Hood who killed twenty-one men in his own brief twenty-one years. But he didn't rob the rich and give his loot to the poor; he probably didn't kill nearly that many men; and he may have been older than twenty-one when he died. Sheriff Garrett had been on the Kid's trail for months when he tracked him to the home of Pete Maxwell, who lived at the old Fort Sumner military post, which the Army had abandoned in the 1860s.

Near midnight on July 14, 1881, the sheriff was in Mr. Maxwell's bedroom, questioning him about the Kid's whereabouts, when the Kid entered the room. Billy, apparently sensing the sheriff's presence in the darkness, asked: *Quien es*? Sheriff Garrett drew his gun and fired twice. The Kid's friends buried him in the old Fort Sumner cemetery beside his comrades O'Folliard and Bowdrie. (The remains of soldiers buried there later were moved to the National Cemetery in Santa Fe, but a few civilians are buried there, some of them recently. One of the graves is Pete Maxwell's. He died in 1898.)

For fifty years only a wooden cross marked Billy's grave, but in the 1930s the large white stone was erected. "Pals" is etched upon it in large letters, above the names of the three outlaws and their death dates. As you face the tombstone, Mr. O'Folliard's grave is on the left, Mr. Bowdrie's in the center, and the Kid's on the right. Unless you believe—as some do—that Sheriff Garrett killed the wrong man and Billy escaped to Hico, Texas, where he was known as "Brushy Bill" Roberts and lived to a ripe old age.

But that's another story.

Lawman Garrett Moved Up After Death

Bryan Woolley

Las Cruces
•

In the tiny Oddfellows Cemetery in Las Cruces is an apparently empty family grave plot with a concrete border. Stamped into the border is the name "Garrett." When Pat Garrett, the slayer of Billy the Kid, was himself murdered in 1908, he was buried here, presumably among other relatives. The barren, dusty graveyard seems an appropriate resting place for a frontier sheriff who died with his boots on. But Pat and the other Garretts buried here were later moved to lovelier quarters in the grassy, tree-shaded Masonic Cemetery across the road.

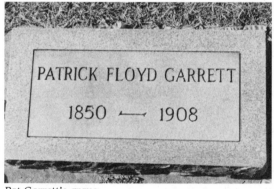

PATRICK FLOYD GARRETT

1850 ⸺ 1908

Pat Garrett's grave

Here he lies, along with his wife Apolinaria and nine other relatives. They share a large family tombstone that reads simply "Garrett," but each grave also has its own smaller stone with name and dates.

There is still at least one interesting grave site in the old Oddfellows Cemetery. Remember Judge Roy Bean, Texas' "Law West of the Pecos"? His brother Sam, who died in 1903, is buried here alongside his family, identified on their stones only as Lupita, Sammy, Dora, Samuel and Mother, who didn't even rate a name. She was born in 1834 and died in 1911.

D. H. Lawrence Shrine Preserves His Memory in New Mexico

Bryan Woolley

Taos •

During the 1920s, the great English author D. H. Lawrence and his wife, Frieda, lived for several years in a small log cabin on a ranch in the mountains north of Taos. There, it is said, he wrote parts of *The Plumed Serpent*. The owner of the ranch, Taos socialite and art patron Mabel Dodge Luhan, tried to make a gift of the ranch to Mr. Lawrence, but he refused it. Frieda accepted it, however, giving Mrs. Luhan the original manuscript of *Sons and Lovers* in return.

Mr. Lawrence, author of *Women in Love*, *Lady Chatterly's Lover* and other classics, died in France in 1930. In 1934, his wife built a small shrine to his memory on a steep mountainside above the cabin where they had lived. The following year, she had Mr. Lawrence's body exhumed and cremated and his ashes shipped to her at Taos. Her plan was to inter them at sunset to the beat of Indian drums, but Mrs. Luhan told the Indians the place was cursed and drove them away. Frieda then suspected that Mrs. Luhan intended to steal the author's ashes and scatter them over the ranch.

To foil her rival's plot, Frieda had the ashes mixed with concrete and molded into a large, immovable block, which she placed inside the shrine. The altarlike block, with the initials D. H. L. on the front and a

crude, gray concrete phoenix on top, is the focal point of the tiny building. In the 1950s, Frieda gave the ranch to the University of New Mexico, which promised to maintain it forever. Upon her death, she was buried near the entrance to the shrine.

Pilgrims from all over the world drive the 4½-mile unpaved ranch road from State Highway 522 and climb the long, zigzag concrete walk up the mountainside to pay homage to the great writer. Over a typical weeklong period, the guest book in the shrine had been signed by visitors from Germany, France, Great Britain, Italy, Haiti, Switzerland, Canada, Greece, New Zealand, Mexico, Norway, Turkey, Australia and perhaps two dozen American states.

(above) D. H. Lawrence shrine
(below) Altarlike block containing Lawrence's ashes with a phoenix on top

Western Legend Kit Carson Rests Quietly in Taos

Bryan Woolley

Ask anyone to name the three greatest American frontiersmen and he is likely to reply: Daniel Boone, Davy Crockett and Kit Carson. Mr. Boone is buried in Kentucky. General Santa Anna cremated Colonel Crockett with the other Alamo defenders in San Antonio. Kit Carson lies in a grave only two blocks from his old adobe home in Taos.

Born in Kentucky in 1809, Kit Carson ran away from his apprenticeship as a saddle maker when he was seventeen and struck out for the Rockies. There he became a sort of frontier Renaissance man. During his forty-year career, he was at various times a fur trapper and mountain man; an interpreter of Indian languages; the guide for John C. Fremont's exploration expedition to California and a participant in the Bear Flag Revolt of 1846, in which Colonel Fremont wrested control of California from Mexico; a rancher; an Indian agent; a Union military officer in the Civil War; and an Indian fighter. Colonel Fremont's best-selling books about these adventures made Kit Carson a household name.

For more than a century he was considered one of the West's greatest heroes. But revisionist historians lately have put him under a cloud of political incorrectness because of his treatment of American Indians, particularly the Navajos, during his Indian-fighting days. He lies beside his wife, Josefa, behind an iron fence erected around their graves by the Masonic

124

Kit Carson's grave at Taos

Grand Lodge of New Mexico in 1908. Kit married Josefa, a member of the prominent Jaramillo family, when she was fourteen, and they had eight children. They also adopted several Indian children. A number of Carson children, grandchildren and other relatives are buried in the adjacent plot. Josefa and Kit died in Fort Lyons, Colorado, in 1868, she in childbirth, he exactly a month later of an aneurysm. She was forty, he was fifty-nine. Their bodies were brought home to Taos a year later. The cemetery in which they lie is now part of the Kit Carson Memorial State Park in downtown Taos.

Many other Taos pioneers, both famous and infamous, are buried there. One of them, Captain Smith H. Simpson, helped Kit and others re-erect the U.S. flag in Taos Plaza after Confederates removed it during the Civil War. Since that day, the U.S. flag has flown day and night in Taos Plaza to commemorate the event. A more recent pioneer of sorts was Mabel Dodge Luhan (1879–1962), a wealthy socialite and patron of the arts who came to Taos from New York in 1916 and remained the rest of her life. The flamboyant Mrs. Luhan had a great impact on the cultural life of Taos and helped establish the town's international fame as an art community. She wrote several books on Taos life and was a philanthropist and friend of many artists and authors, including D. H. Lawrence (see pp. 122–123).

Her surprisingly modest grave is in a quiet corner of the cemetery.

Journalist's Pup Buried in His Yard

Bryan Woolley

Albuquerque

In the side yard of the tiny white frame house at 900 Girard Boulevard S.E. in Albuquerque lies a small tombstone with only one word on it: "Cheetah." The house belonged to America's most famous and beloved war correspondent, Ernie Pyle, and his wife, Jerry. Not long before Mr. Pyle went off to cover World War II, he and Jerry bought the little house, intending to make it their place of peace and refuge after years of journalistic wandering. Cheetah, a Shetland shepherd, was their dog. Ernie had brought her home to Jerry as a gift, and she became a beloved member of their household.

A Japanese sniper killed Ernie Pyle on a Pacific island in 1945. A few months later, Jerry died, too. Neither was buried in Albuquerque. A neighbor took Cheetah in. Several years later, when Cheetah died, the neighbor buried her in the yard of her old home and placed the little stone on her grave.

Grave of Ernie Pyle's dog

The Pyles, who had no children, had willed their little house to the city of Albuquerque to be used as a branch library. It was the Albuquerque Public Library's first branch, and it remains a busy neighborhood library today. A few mementos of Ernie and Jerry Pyle, including a picture of Cheetah, are on display there.

126

Smokey Bear Returned to His Home

Bryan Woolley

Capitan
•

In a tiny state park in the center of the tiny mountain town of Capitan is one of the most famous graves in New Mexico. Almost everyone in America knows who Smokey Bear was, even though they are likely to call him (incorrectly) Smokey the Bear. After a disastrous forest fire in the Capitan Mountains in 1950, firefighters found a 2¹/₂-month-old, four-pound black bear cub clinging to a charred tree. His rescuers named him "Smokey."

When Smokey had recovered from his burns, he was flown to Washington, D.C. There he was given a new home in the National Zoo and was made an ally in the U.S. Forest Service's efforts to educate the public about the prevention of woodland fires. Over the

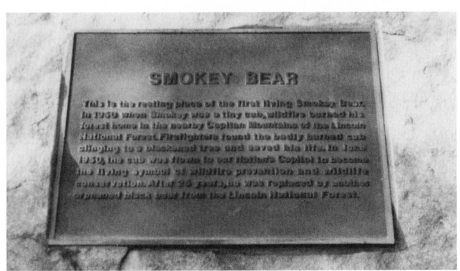

Smokey Bear's grave

years since, Smokey Bear, wearing a forest ranger's hat, and his slogan, "Only You Can Prevent Forest Fires," have become famous the world over.

When Smokey died in 1976, his body was returned to Capitan and buried at Smokey Bear Historical State Park. The park's visitors center includes exhibits about forest fires, a history of the Smokey Bear fire-prevention campaign and a theater. The grounds are landscaped to represent the six vegetation zones of the Capitan area. Smokey is buried under a boulder in a secluded corner of the grounds. A bronze plaque on the rock tells his story.

After Smokey's death, another orphaned black bear from New Mexico's Lincoln National Forest carried on his work.

U.S. Astrochimp Found Peace in N.M.

Bryan Woolley

Alamogordo

The first American to be rocketed into space was Alan Shepard, right? No, it was Ham, the nation's first astrochimp. On January 3, 1961, Ham was strapped into a capsule perched atop an eighty-three-foot-tall Redstone rocket and launched from Cape Canaveral. He reached a top speed of 5,800 mph and an altitude of 155 miles. He was recovered at sea 420 miles down range from the launch site. His suborbital journey lasted about sixteen minutes.

They say Ham was in a really foul mood when he returned, but his trip helped prove man could live and work in space. Ham died in 1983 in his retire-

Ham's plaque at the International Space Hall of Fame in Alamogordo

ment home at the North Carolina Zoological Park. Three months later, he was buried at the foot of the flagpole in front of the International Space Hall of Fame in Alamogordo. A bronze plaque commemorates his extraordinary flight.

See also p. 196 for National Cemeteries in New Mexico.

Oklahoma

Famous Son Will Rogers Returned to Home Soil

Leon Unruh

Claremore

Will Rogers had an amazing resumé. He was born in 1879 in Indian Territory near Oologah in Rogers County, which was named for his father, Clem, a Cherokee senator who owned a 60,000-acre ranch. Will, also part Irish, was a Wild West show cowboy in Argentina and a trick roper in vaudeville, a movie star and a humorist whose populist twist on the news made him the highest-paid radio personality during the Great Depression.

He was a journalist whose last written word was "death," and he died famously when a small plane piloted by his friend Wiley Post crashed near Point Barrow, Alaska, in 1935.

After nine years in storage in Glendale, California, Mr. Rogers' body was brought back to Claremore, Oklahoma, where he had planned to retire on a twenty-acre farm that after his death was turned into the Will Rogers Museum. His terminally ill wife, Betty Blake Rogers, designed the garden under which the Rogers family rests; she died three weeks after Mr. Rogers came home. Joining him in the museum mausoleum are his wife, son Fred (died 1921), daughter Mary (1989) and daughter-in-law Astria (1987).

The boxlike tomb visible in the garden, says museum staff member Jim O'Donnell, "is just a false front." It makes a vaulted ceiling for the mausoleum, which is open only by special request. In the garden a bronze Will Rogers forever rides his horse Soapsuds, a statue identical, Mr. O'Donnell says, to one at Texas Tech University in Lubbock and to another at Will Rogers Coliseum in Fort Worth.

A tall bronze statue inside the museum has long since gone green with age—except for the shoes, which thousands of hands have polished to a gleam. Perhaps it is a fond thank you for his most famous saying, carved into the base: "I never met a man I didn't like."

Will Rogers statue and false crypt in garden at Will Rogers Museum

© Leon Unruh

Cowboy 101: Bulldoggers, Ranchers Head to the Hills When They Pass On

Leon Unruh

Ponca City
Marland

Once upon a time, they were kings of what may have been the most famous ranch north of Texas, the 101. They ran a gigantic spread founded when this was Oklahoma Territory, and they governed a Wild West Show that toured the country. Now these three men lie on Cowboy Hill, a bluff overlooking the Salt Fork of the Arkansas River. They are fenced in.

There is Zack T. Miller (1877–1952), one of the sons of the founder of the 101 Ranch. And Sam Stigall (1885–1967), the "pioneer foreman" who worked from 1902 to 1929. And Jack Webb (1902–1956), whose

Cowboy Hill

Monument for Jack Webb

ornately carved stone reads: "World's Greatest Trick Roper and Sharp Shooter."

"Somebody got a little fanciful," says Mr. Webb's daughter, Jean Evans. Ms. Evans inherited the north-central Oklahoma ranch after her father bought it from the Millers. "There's not that much left of it now," she says.

The ranch's name came from the size of the spread. "It was supposed to be 101,000 acres, but that included a lot of Indian land," Ms. Evans says. George Washington Miller leased the land from the Ponca Indians in 1879 and soon built it into a 160-square-mile empire that attracted nationwide interest and even allowed dude-ranching Easterners to help get those dogies along, for a fee.

The 101 Ranch Wild West Show toured the country from the statehood year of 1907 through 1931. Among its stars was Bill Pickett, a Texas-born black cowboy who had invented bulldogging—originally the practice of biting the steer's lip to help bring it down. After Mr. Pickett was killed in 1922 while breaking a horse on the 101, he was buried on a hill north of Marland; his horse, Spradley, is buried there, too. Travelers along Oklahoma Route 156 north of Marland will soon be able to visit Mr. Pickett's grave, which is being made accessible to the public. Work has begun on a parking lot along the highway and a visitation area at the grave.

Neither Jerry Murphy, a Corpus Christi resident who is an expert on the 101, nor Ms. Evans, knows exactly who is buried on the hill. Ms. Evans thinks it may include an ox driver and some children. Mr. Murphy, whose grandmother was a Cherokee dancer for the 101 Wild West Show and who says he has the world's largest collection of 101 memorabilia, adds that one of the graves may belong to Curbstone Kirby, a show-wagon driver.

Cowboy Hill, where the three ranch men are buried, belongs to the 101 Ranch Oldtimers Association, which meets each August 16 in Ponca City.

"We have quite a few people come to our meetings, but they're getting fewer and fewer," Ms. Evans says.

∞

Ponca City, a few miles north of Marland, is noted for its Pioneer Woman statue, the Marland Mansion and the Conoco refinery. The IOOF cemetery is just west of the refinery on the west side of town. In addition to members of the Marland family, several Grand Army of the Republic veterans are buried here, from the 138th Illinois Cavalry, 72nd New York Infantry and so forth. In the heart of the cemetery are seven stones for British pilots and crewmen who died while training at flight school in Ponca during World War II.

The Oak Grove section, on the cemetery's south side, contains graves displaced from Lucas in 1974 by the construction of Kaw Reservoir.

Battle Sounds Thunder Near Geronimo

Leon Unruh

Lawton

Thirty-odd years after Geronimo's death, invoking his name still inspired soldiers.

"Paratroopers from the 501st Airborne started that back in the early World War II days, and they took Geronimo and his family in as a member of their brigade," says Melvin Kerchee, Jr., who manages the cemetery where Geronimo is buried. Soldiers even helped build the eagle-topped stone monument that sits above Geronimo's grave in an Apache prisoner-of-war cemetery at Fort Sill, near Lawton in southwestern Oklahoma.

Geronimo's monument

Although his birthdate is lost, Geronimo is thought to have been at least eighty years old when he died of pneumonia in February 1909. Born near what is now Clifton, Arizona, he was named Goyahkla (One Who Yawns). In her book *Geronimo*, historian Angie Debo says he got his better-known name during a battle with Mexican soldiers who were frightened by his skill:

"Each time he emerged, the Mexicans began to cry out in terror, 'Cuidado! Watch out! Geronimo!' (Perhaps this was as close as they could come to the choking sounds that composed his name, or perhaps they were calling on St. Jerome.) The Apaches took it up as their battle cry, and Goyahkla became Geronimo." Geronimo and his band fought American intruders until they were hunted down by the U.S. Cavalry in Mexico in 1886. The government packed them off to humid, malaria-ridden Alabama and Florida, where a number died. The government relented and, in 1894, let them move back west, not to the desert, but to southwestern Oklahoma Territory, where Fort Sill stood on the semi-arid plains within sight of the Wichita Mountains.

Geronimo's later years were spent farming, selling his violent story to newspapers and customers at exhibitions, and drinking. He was a regular inside the limestone walls of the Fort Sill guardhouse. He was hired as an Indian scout, a job that entailed transporting rations to feed the Indians.

He died after fifteen years at the post. Ms. Debo writes of Geronimo's funeral:

> Just before the grave was filled, the relatives of the dead leader solemnly placed his riding whip and blanket in it. Before he died, he had told them to tie his horse to a certain tree and to hang up his belongings on the east side of the grave, and in three days he would come and get them, but his widow decided to bury his possessions with him.

Although military cemeteries officially are known only as post cemeteries or prisoner-of-war cemeteries, this one is known locally as Geronimo Cemetery, Mr. Kerchee says. Two other POW graveyards, carrying the tribal names Bailtso and Chihuahua, are close by. Three hundred and forty Apache prisoners are buried in the three cemeteries. Most of the remaining Apaches left the post after the government granted them amnesty in 1913 (freeing up land for artillery training), but forty-two dependents still asked to be buried there.

Prompted by two 1993 movies about Geronimo's life, "a lot of his descendants visit his grave and those of the other relatives," Mr. Kerchee says. Visitors often leave a token at the grave or in a "gift tree." The gifts were left, Mr. Kerchee says, in the belief "the spirit never dies, and from time to time the spirit returns." Well-wishers at Geronimo's stone monument have tied feathers and pouches to boughs in a cedar tree. On one

Military cemetery

November day, the monument itself held gifts of a geode, quartz, leather strips, a quarter, a nickel, nineteen pennies and one Chuck E Cheese token.

Buried alongside Geronimo are his first wife Zi-Yeh (1869–1904), daughters Eva Geronimo Godeley (1889–1911) and Lulu Geronimo (1865–1898), and son Fenton Geronimo, who died in 1897. Befitting his status, Geronimo's rock-and-mortar marker is large and has a cast-concrete eagle on top, with the simplest of inscriptions: "Geronimo." Stones of the other Apaches, even the Warm Springs band's Chief Loco, are government-issue white tablets. Many stones list family ties—son of, wife of, brother of—but a few say something on the order of, "Dah-ke-ya, Apache warrior with Geronimo, 1861–1899."

Fort Sill's role in the long war against the Indians is over, but the sounds of battle still thunder across these plains. Soldiers at Fort Sill, the home of the Army Artillery and Missile Center, regularly take target practice with 105mm and 155mm howitzers—big self-propelled guns that shake the earth. On a quiet day at Geronimo's grave, visitors can hear the shells whipping through the sky and their distant report.

To find Geronimo Cemetery, enter via Key Gate on Interstate 44. The post is always open. Stay to the right and look for brown signs leading to Geronimo's grave.

The simplicity of the country cemeteries, along a creek in the grassy hills, differs from the post cemetery in "downtown" Fort Sill. A certain area—Chiefs' Knoll—within the 5,350-grave post cemetery is reserved for historical purposes. It holds the remains of twenty-three chiefs, eleven black soldiers from the 10th Cavalry who arrived and died in 1869, and assorted settlers.

Among the best known are Settain-te (Satanta, or White Bear), the unrepentant Kiowa leader, (see also p. 34), and Quanah Parker, the last

Chief Satanta's monument

© Leon Unruh

Comanche chief, who adapted quite nicely to the white man's ways after surrendering in 1875 and moving his followers to the Comanche-Kiowa reservation at Fort Sill. Ranching and investment were good to him. When Parker died at his ranch in 1911, *The New Handbook of Texas* says, he was perhaps the wealthiest Indian in the country. After robbers ransacked his grave, he was reburied at a mission cemetery; when the army wanted that land for a missile base, he was buried again, this time in 1957 at Fort Sill with his legendary mother, Cynthia Ann Parker, and his little sister.

Artillery and missiles aside, Fort Sill is quiet and pretty and something of an open-air museum. Trees line the parade square, a long line of historical howitzers is open for review, and the limestone headquarters building with the wheeled gun out front is a perfect backdrop to the nation's flag. It is the kind of place where a child—of the age at which he might yell "Geronimo!" while jumping off his porch—runs to salute the colors as they're lowered under the red November sky.

∞

The small town of Geronimo, south of Lawton, has no cemetery.

In the Walters city cemetery, south of Lawton on I-44, then east on Oklahoma Highway 53, the wind is not the only thing sweeping 'cross the plain. There is music as well. Gentle religious melodies emanate from the Hertzler Memorial, towering above the willows lining a pond where ducks and geese swim in artistic harmony.

Laughter, Singing and Shame Echo Through Tulsa's Cemeteries

Leon Unruh

Tulsa

Memorial Park Cemetery has 54,000 graves on 260 acres, linked by eighteen miles of roads. Twenty-one employees trim the shrubs, open and close graves and set the stones. This is a big-time cemetery. Here you will find the Garden of the Apostles and the Garden of the Prophets and an extensive mausoleum. There are stone bridges, a few trees and wide-open views unhindered by many upright stones in this busy corner of southeast Tulsa.

"You have to own six or eight spaces to own a monument," says Jason Thames, the chief sexton, who at this enormous graveyard has the title of Park Superintendent.

Memorial Park's most famous occupants are singer Bob Wills and comedian Sam Kinison. "Both of them have flat markers," says Mr. Thames without looking it up. "Bob Wills' marker is granite, and Sam Kinison's is bronze." Mr. Kinison (1953–92) lies in section twenty-eight. Mr. Wills (1905–75), in section fifteen, is "quite frequently visited," but personal gifts are never left.

Memorial Park does not cater to specialized groups, Mr. Thames says. "The only different section we would have is for the American Legion." Unlike some large cemeteries, Memorial Park does not have shops for flowers or gifts. "The only thing that we offer is a chapel for the services," Mr. Thames says.

Are there ever any social events, such as weddings, on the parklike grounds?

"I heard once upon a time they did have them in the chapel."

The best thing about Memorial Park, Mr. Thames says, is the automatic chime tower near the gate in the northwest corner, where a funeral procession would arrive.

"When more than three cars drive through, the chimes will play 'Amazing Grace.'"

Cemetery hours are 7 A.M. to 7 P.M. After that, the gates are locked.

Without a decent burial

In 1921, Tulsa was an oil boom town with a spectacular future. Then, as with other cities in those strident years of race-baiting and anti-communist witch hunts, Tulsa suffered from a race riot remarkable for the extent of damage and the number of deaths, which may have been more than 300.

The three-day riot was ignited when blacks and whites clashed outside the city jail, where an African-American was being held on what turned out to be spurious charges. Even today, there are no sure numbers of black or white dead. Until Scott Ellsworth published *Death in a Promised Land* in 1982, no one said much about the riots.

Mechelle Brown of Tulsa's Greenwood Cultural Center says, "It's not in any history book in any of our classrooms. The only way we found out about it is what our parents handed down."

Recently, whites and blacks have come together to learn about the riot and try to heal wounds. The victims, ignored for so many years, are being remembered. Although many black Tulsans have been laid to rest in one old city cemetery at 11th Street and Peoria and in another, Crown Hill, on East Pine, don't expect to find many riot victims. A man in his nineties has spoken of how he was sent through the streets to collect bodies in his truck.

"There was many, many people whose bodies were thrown in the river or didn't get a decent burial," Ms. Brown says.

Robber's Tour Ended in Guthrie

Leon Unruh

Guthrie

The long purgatory of train robber Elmer McCurdy began in October 1911, when a posse shot him dead in the Osage Hills of Oklahoma. More than six decades later, he was put in the ground with considerably more pomp than he might have gotten originally. That first fall, an undertaker embalmed the infamous outlaw so thoroughly that the funeral parlor in Pawhuska was able to prop him up and attract visitors from far away, according to Richard J. Basgall in *The Career of Elmer McCurdy, Deceased*.

After four years, he was taken west by a touring show and ended up as a real mummy in a Los Angeles wax museum. He variously portrayed an outlaw and drug addict, and he even had a role in the movie *She Freak* before he was covered with fluorescent paint and left for dead, so to speak, at a fun house called Laff in the Dark. The fact he was real became known after a prop man for the *Six Million Dollar Man* accidentally pulled the stiff's arm off.

Detective work traced his origins to Oklahoma. It was decided he would be buried in Summit View Cemetery north of Guthrie,

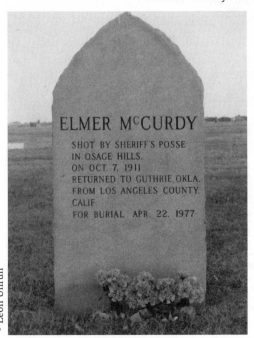

Monument of Elmer McCurdy

© Leon Unruh

joining the territorial fathers and mothers. He was brought back in 1977 and given a sober funeral in a pine box, attended by a hundred or so. Concrete was poured over his coffin to ensure the end of his saga. He lies next to another slain outlaw, Bill Doolin, a bank robber prominent in Kansas and Oklahoma.

Guthrie itself was no shrinking violet in the early days after the land rush of 1889. This boomtown thirty miles north of Oklahoma City was the first state capital. Leftovers include the giant Scottish Rite Masonic Temple (the original capitol), Victorian mansions and 1,600 acres of city land listed in the National Historic Register.

Some cemetery occupants were well thought of. Among them is Robert Martin (1833–97). He was secretary of the Territory of Oklahoma 1890–93, acting governor 1891–92, and Guthrie mayor 1894–96. He died ten years before statehood.

"I love working out here: beaucoups of history," says groundskeeper Steve Calvert. The touch of history spreads here like afternoon shadows, creeping across every stone on these gentle hills. A sunset drive leads to the grave of Ashley Megan Eckels: Born July 25, 1990; died on the morning of April 19, 1995, in the Oklahoma City bombing. An angel kneels eternally on Ashley's heart-shaped tombstone and a teddy bear with matted fur leans outward from its mooring. It is a small gesture to straighten the bear, but a sad gesture, here among the rectangular stones of grandparents.

They Rest Under God's Big Top

Kathryn Straach

Hugo
•

Children squeal with laughter on the playground at the nearby elementary school. The sound is appropriate as it echoes across the Showman's Rest area of Mount Olivet Cemetery. Many circus performers and employees are buried here. If it is possible for a cemetery to be fun, this one's special section would qualify. The Al G. Kelly and Miller Brothers Circus wintered in the Hugo area for several years. Showman's Rest was started in the 1960s when the Elephant Man (a.k.a. John Carroll) established a trust fund.

Stand here long enough and you can almost hear the organ grinder, smell the popcorn and see the trapeze artists fly by. The personalities of those who have died, and for some who are merely on the lineup, come across in the markers.

In the center is a tall monument that reads, "A Tribute to All Showmen Under God's Big Top." It features an elephant standing on its back legs and a circus tent. Another tall marker belongs to Big John Strong, known as Tall Grass Showman. His likeness is carved into the nine-foot memorial. The back reads, "Peace Be

Monument of Big John Strong

With You Big John/The Man With More Friends Than Santa Claus." Nearby stands a wagon-wheel monument belonging to Ted Bowman. It states, "There's Nothing Left But Empty Popcorn Sacks and Wagon Tracks. The Circus is Gone."

William Woodcock's marker reads, "A-1 Elephant trainer at rest." Harry Rooks' says, "A life long circus performer, aerialist and horse trainer," and it features a horse on both sides.

John Narfski's is etched with a hippo. Zefta Loyal was "Queen of the Bareback Riders," and "Beloved Mother of Dolly and Gina." Peggy Fournier—"Aunt Peggy"—seems to be the only unhappy one. Her headstone reads, "I Would Rather Be in California."

In addition to circus people, the cemetery has a section with world-champion rodeo cowboys, including Todd Whatley, Freckles Brown and Lane Frost, whose life was featured in the movie *8 Seconds*. Also, William Edmond Ansley, better known as Buster Brown of Buster Brown Shoes fame, is buried here. Native-stone walls line the entrance to this beautifully shaded cemetery on rolling land. The neatly laid out cemetery celebrated its ninetieth anniversary in March 1998.

To get to the cemetery, take U.S. 271 to exit U.S. 70 East. Travel about one mile until you get to Hugo Elementary and turn left.

See also p. 196 for the National Cemetery in Oklahoma.

Arkansas

A Sculptural Tour of Arkansas

Leon Unruh

© Leon Unruh

If you are looking for the best funerary art-work Arkansas has to offer, the Historic Preservation Program makes it easy. The program collected information on sculptures—from Confederate monuments to giant bugs to cemetery angels—from across the state and published descriptions and locations in a dandy fold-out brochure called *Stone & Steel, A Sculptural Tour of Arkansas.*

Copies of the brochure are available from the program's office: 1500 Tower Building, 323 Center Street, Little Rock, Arkansas 72201; (501) 324-9880. They may also be available at tourist-information booths.

Mount Holly Cemetery Reigns in Arkansas

Leon Unruh

Little Rock

Mention Mount Holly Cemetery, and you will almost always get the response: "The Westminster Abbey of Arkansas." If a statuary fan mentions it to Mark Christ of the State Department of Arkansas Heritage, you will hear: "That's your holy grail."

"It's got everything," he says.

It certainly has name recognition. The cemetery just south of downtown Little Rock holds ten governors, thirteen state Supreme Court justices, five Confederate generals, twenty-one mayors of Little Rock and assorted editors, military heroes, doctors and lawyers. For instance, there is Edward N. Weigel, who discovered bauxite, or aluminum ore, in Arkansas. There is also a Texan named David O. Dodd, "the Boy Martyr of the Confederacy," who got hanged in 1864 for not telling the Union forces who gave him secret information.

And there is Quatie, the Cherokee chief's wife whose trail of tears ended here in 1839. Originally buried near the Arkansas River, she was moved to a burial ground downtown and finally up the hill to Mount Holly, where the surroundings were more noble and the funerary statuary is as good as it gets. Visitors to the 5,000-grave cemetery at Interstate 630 and Broadway will immediately notice the draped columns and the statues of little girls, especially angel-escorted Mary Watkins and the Basham girls in fine Italian marble. Look a little harder for the Henry C. Brookin

© Leon Unruh

(above) Mary Watkins'
monument
(right) Henry C. Brookin
firefighting monument

© Leon Unruh

monument—a firefighter eternally ready (let us hope he is not fighting fire eternally)—and for Booker Worthen's stone, which sports herbs because Mr. Worthen was a horticulturist.

Not long ago, horticulture, so to speak, dominated the grounds. Steven Adams, the sexton, remembered youthful nighttime visits to the cemetery—"It was like being in the forest"—but the underbrush and transients were cleared out a few years ago by work-release crews. This was overseen by the seventeen women of the Mount Holly Cemetery Association. Peg Smith, a member of the association for forty years, tells how the capital city had a common burial ground downtown until 1843, when U.S. Senator Chester Ashley and Roswell Beebe gave the city four square blocks "to dignify things." Beebe, who died in 1856 after gaining a reputation as a railroad promoter, at one point held title to all of Little Rock.

The city ran the cemetery until 1877, when a group of five men took over its maintenance. "In 1915, seventeen women said the men were not doing a good job" and took it over as volunteers. "I would guess half the people at City Hall don't even know it belongs to the city," Ms. Smith says.

The cemetery, the resting place for Arkansas' old money families, has a black section. In addition, "Many black people are buried throughout the cemetery because their masters would sometimes bury their servants with them," she says.

There used to be more Catholics and Jews buried here, she says, but their families moved many of them to religious cemeteries (for example, Calvary and the Jewish section of Oakland Cemetery) as they opened. Coincidentally, the flashpoint of Arkansas desegregation was just a few blocks west of here, at Central High School.

Perhaps because she spends so much time in Mount Holly leading schoolchildren on tours, Ms. Smith knows the place inside and out. As evidence, she mentions she has found fourteen typographical errors, including a faulty attempt at founder Roswell Beebe's name.

Ms. Smith praises a Dallas woman, Sybil Crawford, for her definitive book, *Jubilee*, which commemorated Mount Holly's 150th year. That book, as well as an index of the buried, is available for purchase. The cemetery also produces a brochure showing the location and pedigree of many of its occupants.

And if you are looking for a final resting place with a nice Victorian touch, you might consider Mount Holly. There are some places left.

∞

Little Rock National Cemetery, southeast of downtown near the airport, was first an occupation campground for Union troops, then a cemetery for them. Later, Union remains were brought in from across the state for reburial, and room was granted for a Confederate cemetery, laid out on the southern side of the acreage. Among the reburied dead were 640 moved from Mount Holly Cemetery. There are now well over 20,000 veterans and dependents in the cemetery, at Confederate Boulevard and East 26th Street.

Next door to the north is Oakland Cemetery, a large, slightly worn but beautiful burying ground. It has some fascinating sculptures and mausoleums.

© Leon Unruh

Little Rock National Cemetery

Fayetteville Area Has Veterans from Many U.S. Wars

Leon Unruh

When the Civil War ended in 1865, battle dead were buried all over northwest Arkansas. Two fighting grounds in the northwestern corner of the state were at Pea Ridge, northeast of Rogers, and Prairie Grove, southwest of Fayetteville.

Fayetteville National Cemetery

It wasn't until 1867, when Fayetteville National Cemetery was opened, that an effort was made to collect the dead from battlefields around the area and re-inter them on federal property. "After the Civil War, the government paid people to dig them up and bring them up to Fayetteville," says Milo Cumpston, who has taken a paternal interest in the city's military graveyards. The pay was fifty cents to a dollar per corpse. The Union dead and the Unknowns, totaling 2,059, were laid to rest within the brick walls of the National Cemetery south of downtown.

The National Cemetery now contains veterans of every conflict but the Revolutionary War. And there is a slight chance that may change. Some Revolutionary War veterans were given bonus land in northwest Arkansas, says Bruce Schaffer, the cemetery representative, and there are several small cemeteries locally where they are buried.

One is on Pumphouse Road south of town in an area becoming an industrial district. Its humble stones are fenced in; no sign points to it. One stone indicates a death in 1835. Mr. Cumpston, a Marine who served in the Pacific theater during World War II, led a drive to reinter those veterans in the national cemetery.

"We found a great number of them that had pre-Revolutionary War birthdates. And then we got into the National Archives and confirmed it," he says.

At least one family resisted the proposal, however, so it is on hold. A monument at the National Cemetery, near West 15th Street and School Avenue, stands in for the Revolutionary War veterans.

After the War of Northern Aggression was settled in most minds, Confederate families took an oak-covered hillside on Fayetteville's East Rock Street and buried their own, who came mostly from Texas, Arkansas, Missouri and Louisiana. (Some Confederate States Army veterans who survived the war also were buried here.) Each state is represented by a branch of the "Deo Vindice" Confederate cross, a design of graves radiating from the monument erected in 1897. It is an attractive and moving place.

The monument reads:

These were men
Whom power could not corrupt,
Whom death could not terrify,
Whom defeat could not dishonor.

Oak and Evergreen Cemeteries

Immediately south of the National Cemetery lies Oak Cemetery. Several occupants were born before Emancipation, and one has to wonder how much of what is now open land is underlain by graves whose markers have been lost to time. A great cultural distance away—but not more than a couple miles—is Evergreen Cemetery, which has Fayetteville's finest collection of old stones but because it adjoins the University of Arkansas campus is often used as an informal parking lot. Senator J. William Fulbright, who created the famous scholarship program, is buried here. Another politician with international interests was Archibald Yell.

Mr. Yell was born in North Carolina in 1797, fought in the Battle of New Orleans, was the first member of Congress from Arkansas after statehood arrived in 1836, and its first governor. After returning to Congress, he resigned to become a colonel in the Arkansas Volunteers in the Mexican War of 1846. He was killed at Buena Vista in 1847.

The family of Lafayette Gregg lost a nine-month-old in 1864, apparently while Daddy, who later became a state Supreme Court justice, was away at war. "Dear Alice, Death's first claim on the family," the stone reads. "A sweet babe lost to us and a little seraph added to the halls of heaven."

∞

Southwest of Fayetteville along the U.S. 71 Bypass is Dowell Cemetery, a rural graveyard. It was first used around the turn of the century, and many of its earliest occupants were children. A Thompson stone asks, "How many hopes lie buried here?" Ten miles south of Fayetteville on U.S. 71 in Greenland, the graceful Baptist Ford Church has a cemetery adjacent.

In Bentonville, thirty miles north of Fayetteville, look for the grave of Wal-Mart founder Sam Walton in the city cemetery on Southwest F Street near Wal-Mart headquarters.

Arkansas Minister Lies near Statue of Christ

Leon Unruh

Eureka Springs

It took a confident man to build a seven-story statue of Jesus Christ and perhaps a humble one to have himself entombed at the statue's feet. Gerald L. K. Smith fancied himself that man.

The Reverend Smith and his wife, Elna M. Robe Smith, lie in a granite tomb under the outstretched left arm of the Christ of the Ozarks statue overlooking Eureka Springs, an hour's drive east of Fayetteville. A million tourists enter the parking lot each year, and probably most walk past the grave for a frontal view of the concrete Jesus, but it is doubtful many of them remember the Reverend Smith, a third-generation min-

Christ of the Ozarks

158

ister in the Christian Church and a staunchly conservative orator and lecturer whose greatest days were in the 1950s.

"He certainly had a great burden for our country and had a great concern that our country would turn from its Christian foundation," says Marvin Peterson, interim co-director of the foundation that oversees the property.

While visiting great churches and war monuments across the country, Mr. Peterson says, the Reverend Smith got the idea for a monument to Christ. After the Smiths retired to the healing-waters resort town of Eureka Springs in the 1960s, they got the entrepreneurial ball rolling. The Christ of the Ozarks statue, about seventy feet high and sixty-five feet wide from fingertip to fingertip, was dedicated in 1966. The next phase in the project opened two years later as the *Great Passion Play*, an homage to the *Passion Play* of Oberammergau in Bavaria.

The million-pound Christ of the Ozarks has an undeniably serene and inscrutable countenance. Crowds or no, all-weather loudspeakers broadcast hymns along the lines of "Take It to the Lord in Prayer," to a counterpoint of donkeys braying in the operation's barnyard.

"It's worship-type background music," Mr. Peterson says, "to create an atmosphere of meditation and prayer."

The Reverend Smith died in 1976. His wife died five years later.

∞

Not all of Eureka Springs is buried in the style of the Smiths. Since the 1880s, nearly everybody else has gone to Founders Cemetery, just east of the intersection of U.S. 62 and Passion Play Road. Fred Hopkins has worked for the cemetery for a dozen years, selling plots and staking and marking the graves. Also a teacher at the middle school, he takes his students every year to the cemetery to explore and try their hand at gravestone rubbings. The cemetery, one of the flatter areas in the hill-hugging town, has about thirty-five acres, he says, and 2,000 to 2,500 graves.

It is really a park. Below the cemetery is a pond and waterfall. Locals go for walks on the grounds and teach their children to drive on the serpentine streets. Under the loblolly canopy are graves that reflect Eureka Springs' free-thinking heritage. For example, one plot has an Indian monument of lashed-together cedar poles with a little platform over a girl's grave. A few graves are decorated with chunks of the area's trademark quartz.

"They were laid in by hand and cemented," Mr. Hopkins says. "They're moss-covered, but you can see the crystals."

Angels Fill Eclectic Burial Ground in Fort Smith

Leon Unruh

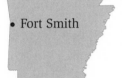

• Fort Smith

Not long ago, a sweet-gum tree broke off at Forest Park Cemetery.

"A lot of people had bought plots to be near the tree," says Michael Kalb, the cemetery manager, "and we didn't want it to go to waste." So the privately owned cemetery had chain-saw artist Scott Winford carve a towering, although slender, angel out of the trunk. And that fitted right in with this eclectic cemetery just south of the Arkansas River. A gypsy king is buried here. A group of Confederate soldiers is interred in a circle. A life-size copy of Rodin's sculpture *The Thinker*, from his work *The Gates of Hell*, sits atop James Stiles' 1977 gravestone. It is anatomically correct and faces Midland Boulevard.

© Leon Unruh

Angel carved from a sweet-gum tree

"Every now and then, somebody puts a ball cap on him," Mr. Kalb says with a laugh.

Lindy Kotner, whose family owns the cemetery, says Mr. Stiles approached his father about ordering the Italian marble statue, but he did not have a place to put it. The senior Kotner offered Mr. Stiles a free grave if he would put it in Forest Park. "His wife didn't want to be here. She thought it was atrocious," Mr. Kotner says. Now, however, she does lie nearby.

On the west side of the cemetery are two poignant remembrances of childhood. Outside the Caldwell mausoleum is a bronze statue of an enraptured girl, lifting off her tiptoes like a sprite in the wind.

"Mr. Caldwell is buried there with three of his wives, or two; we're not sure," Mr. Kotner says.

Down the road a bit is the grave of young Dustin Dickey, who died in 1995. His grave and the headstone he shares with his mother (who is alive) are decorated with dozens of angelic miniatures and a handful of bouquets. Signs at the front corners of the plot read: "Dustin No Fear" and "Mama's Special Boy."

"His mother used to clean the office for the people who owned the cemetery," Mr. Kalb says. "We usually don't allow that [such decorations], but because we knew his mother, we let her do that." Schoolchildren come on Dustin's birthday and death anniversary to remember him. He was thirteen years old and died of an asthma attack.

The King of All Gypsies, Yanko Urich, died in the 1920s. His fol-

© Leon Unruh

(above) Copy of Rodin's The Thinker *atop James Stiles' grave*
(below) Statue at the Caldwell mausoleum

© Leon Unruh

© Leon Unruh

(above) Dustin Dickey's grave
(below) James and Felicity Reynolds monument

© Leon Unruh

lowers, Mr. Kotner says, gave him a big send-off. "When they buried him, they threw gold coins into the grave. And for thirty days later, they guarded the grave to make sure people didn't dig the coins up," he says.

∞

Busy Fort Smith National Cemetery rests downtown on the grounds of the original Fort Smith, a 1817 outpost built to assert U.S. power between the Osages and Cherokees. Among the dead is "hanging judge" Isaac Parker, who sentenced 151 men to die. There also is a cluster of 1850s stones, including a mother and child. Many of the dead being buried these days served at Fort Chaffee southeast of town.

Oak Cemetery, at Greenwood and Dodson streets in central Fort Smith, has a nice collection of statuary. Among the pieces are a trumpet-toting angel atop the stone of David Elbert Dinsmore and a statue on the James and Felicity Reynolds plot—"Lest We Forget," featuring two women helping a wounded Confederate soldier. Mr. Reynolds, who served in the 30th Mississippi Regiment, was seventeen when the Civil War ended.

President's Roots and His Mother Lie Quietly in Hope

Leon Unruh

I stood where the president stood. I tried to imagine the blend of emotions he must feel when he stands at the small iron fence and reads his mother's simple grave marker.

"Virginia Clinton Kelley June 6, 1923 / January 6, 1994," it reads. "Beloved mother of President William Jefferson Clinton and Roger Cassidy Clinton."

Bill Clinton and I are not the only ones to pause here. No matter which way the political winds blow, the crowds keep coming to Hope, a crossroads along Interstate 30 in western Arkansas that makes a lot of hay out of being Clinton's birthplace. Many of the visitors, after touring the downtown museum and the family home, want to see where the entertaining Mrs. Kelley was buried.

"It really was kind of bad for a while. There were people in there from everywhere," says Mary Nell Turner, a member of the Rose Hill Cemetery Association. The association eventually put up signs because cemetery workers would tell visitors where the grave was and would

Grave of Virginia Clinton Kelley

end up chatting for hours. "We decided it was a discreet way of telling them where it was without screaming," she says.

Mrs. Turner, a former high-school journalism teacher, wrote the history of more than a hundred cemeteries for the Hempstead County genealogical society.

Rose Hill, known originally as Cave Hill Cemetery and located north of downton, included sections for white and black citizens. In 1919, the white "front" part became known as Rose Hill (or Rosehill, depending on which map you follow). Visitors are welcomed inside the gate by the Battle family monument, upon which a morose young woman grieves. Near it is the McLarty crypt, holding the forebears of Thomas Franklin "Mack" McLarty III, President Clinton's first chief of staff. The family's wealth came from selling cars, Mrs. Turner says.

High above the grave of county judge Arthur A. Gibson is a heavily draped female figure, bought by the family through a company in St. Louis. Captain Judson T. West, housed in a stone mausoleum with his family, was born in Ohio in 1836 and was a Mississippi River pilot between St. Louis and New Orleans; Samuel Clemens is said to have been a cabin boy on one of his vessels. Captain West went west to Hope in 1874, was president of the first bank, and owned ice, coal and handle-making companies. "He was really a wheeler-dealer," Mrs. Turner says.

© Leon Unruh

Battle family monument

The McRae family is remembered with a small forest of tall stones. One of their relations was Arkansas governor. "They had a beautiful home," Mrs. Turner says. "I don't know how they made their money."

Virginia Kelley lies inside the fence with her first husband, William Jefferson Blythe, and her ice-man father and nurse mother, Eldridge and Edith Cassidy. They moved into Hope during the Great Depression, having lived along Bodcau Branch and earlier in Alabama. After Mr. Blythe's death in an auto accident in 1946, she moved the family to Hot Springs.

One morning at Rose Hill, Robin Lee of the Herndon Funeral Home (celebrating 100 years in business), was taking down a canopy from a funeral the day before. He was in a hurry, so he loosened posts and ropes as he spoke. Most of the graves here, he says, are dug by a fellow who uses a Bobcat to keep his farm clean. "A lot of guys who operate chicken houses also dig graves," he explains. The holes are eight feet by forty inches by five feet deep. Arkansas law requires eighteen inches of solid dirt atop the vault.

"There are still a couple of black cemeteries out in the county, where the relatives and local men, when they have a service, go out there and dig it and cover it up."

There are not many variations in services, he says.

"Cremation hasn't caught on yet," he says. "This is still the South, and people are slow to change their ways."

Memory Gardens

Sitting out past the sale barn east of town on U.S. 67, Memory Gardens is a private cemetery. Here lies Vince Foster—Vincent Walker Foster, Jr.— under a flat granite marker near his parents' graves in the southeast corner. Mr. Foster, who was a deputy White House counsel, committed suicide in 1993 in Washington. The Fosters came from Virginia in the 1830s, Mrs. Turner says. "They were all plantation people" living near the Red River. Vince Foster, Sr., was a real-estate man, and Vince, Jr., went to school with Mrs. Turner's children.

"He was just the idol of all the kids," she says.

Washington Pioneer Cemetery

The settlement of Washington, six miles north of Hope on pretty Arkansas 4, was where Texans frequently met and Jim Bowie's famous knife was created. During the Civil War, it was the Arkansas capital while Union soldiers occupied Little Rock. This flower-laden town, now known as Old Washington State Park, has the state's oldest Methodist Church, formed in 1821.

Pioneer Cemetery, in a vale on the far edge of town, has fifty or so slanted stones dating to at least 1828. After the 1860s, most of the new burials were made in the town's Presbyterian cemetery. Three Revolutionary War veterans were reburied in Pioneer Cemetery in the 1930s by the Daughters of the American Revolution.

See also p. 196 for a listing of National Cemeteries in Arkansas.

Louisiana

New Orleans' Past Is Paydirt

Larry Bleiberg

New
Orleans •

Few other cities in the world have gotten so much mileage out of their dead. In New Orleans, cemeteries are a tourist industry—featured in movies and novels and, unfortunately, crime reports. Some of the most popular cemeteries are in dangerous neighborhoods. Fortunately, a selection of tour companies is ready to escort visitors through these famous cities of the dead. One dependable firm is Historic New Orleans Walking Tours, owned by the author of two books on cemeteries; (504) 947-2120.

New Orleans' oldest standing cemetery, St. Louis No. 1, is the most popular. On the edge of the French

St. Louis No. 1 is New Orleans' oldest and most popular cemetery.

Quarter, this was once the outskirts of town. The tombs were built above ground, guides say, because New Orleans is below sea level, and floods would wash caskets and bodies out of the ground.

Another reason for the unique cemeteries is the practice of reusing and renting tombs. Some tombs contain as many as several dozen family members. Bodies decay quickly in New Orleans heat and humidity. A year after burial, the remains can be placed to the side, making room for a new coffin. Throughout the city, visitors will note several types of tombs. Wall vaults extend in long rows like wood-burning ovens. Family tombs, or mausoleums, stand like small homes. And society tombs are large monuments used by immigrant groups or social organizations to inter their members.

The most famous grave here is believed to belong to Marie Laveau, the voodoo queen of New Orleans. Her tomb is a shrine now. A recent visit found a pile of sheet music and several pennies deposited at its base. It is also covered with X's, which have been scratched on the marble with brick. Many visitors have taken brick from an adjacent tomb, nearly destroying it. The tomb-marking practice is of questionable authenticity—it didn't begin until the 1960s or early 1970s, a century after Ms. Laveau's death.

Grave of voodoo queen Marie Laveau

But there is plenty of authentic history nearby. World-champion chess master Paul Morphy is buried here. A child genius, he gained a worldwide reputation for his playing ability. At age twenty-one, he beat the reigning world champion in Europe. He returned to New Orleans, where he slipped into mental illness and died a recluse.

There is also Homer Plessy, a black man who made history in 1892 when he boarded a whites-only streetcar and demanded to be arrested. The resulting case, Plessy v. Ferguson, went to the U.S. Supreme Court, which found against Mr. Plessy. The justices used the case to construct the "separate but equal" doctrine that justified legal segregation.

And do not forget Bernard De Marginy. Heir to an aristocratic Creole family, he was once one of the wealthiest men on the continent, but he died one of the poorest. Among other things, he is noted for bringing the game of craps to America. As you leave, note the tall monument with angels. This tomb, owned by the Italian Mutual Benevolent Society, found fame when it was climbed and caressed by an LSD-addled Peter Fonda during a sex- and drug-fueled scene in the movie, *Easy Rider*. The archdiocese has since refused to open its property to filmmakers.

But one cemetery that has made the movies is Lafayette No. 1. It is in the Garden District, home to horror novelist Anne Rice. This cemetery is where Tom Cruise emerged from his tomb in the film, *Interview with the Vampire*. It is also home to the title characters in Ms. Rice's Mayfair Witches novels.

Once unkept and unsafe, Lafayette No. 1 has been largely restored through the work of a local preservation group, Save Our Cemeteries, which offers tours (1-888-721-7493). Here, you can catch a glimpse of nineteenth-century New Orleans life. Family tombs are marked with several dozen names, and several hold the remains of mistresses, whose statuses are clearly identified.

They Can't Take It with Them, So They Spend It on the Grave

Larry Bleiberg

Metairie

When Mark Twain quipped that New Orleans' most notable architecture was in its cemeteries, he had to be talking about Metairie. This grandiose graveyard features elaborate architectural statements, modeled on pyramids, cathedrals and other flights of fancy that beg description—and price tags. Rob Florence, author of *New Orleans Cemeteries*, calls Metairie the most beautiful cemetery in the country.

The graveyard also is very easy to visit. The staff lends out cassettes and tape players, which guide drivers through the strange and striking landscape. Check at the administration building; hours are 8 A.M. to 3 P.M.; (504) 486-6331.

Visitors soon discover the 150-acre graveyard holds some wild tales. First off, there is its oval shape, which speaks to the grounds' earlier life as a race-track. It has been said that one of the cemetery's founders built the graveyard out of spite in

1872 because the racing club would not accept him as a member.

But do not forget the graves themselves. Take the tomb of Joseph "Never Smile" Harrington. The statue of a lonely woman stands outside his grandiose marble-lined mausoleum. Mr. Harrington was a widely successful gambler. The female figure is said to be Lady Luck herself.

Another tomb once held Josie Arlington, a famous New Orleans madam. For several years her grave glowed with the reflection of a nearby traffic signal, bathing her resting place with the glow of a red light. The tomb has a statue of a woman outside; some say it is Ms. Arlington trying to get into heaven, others propose that it is a virgin being turned away from a bordello because Ms. Arlington claimed no woman ever lost her virginity at one of her establishments. Many stories told of hauntings at the tomb. Eventually Ms. Arlington was moved to another burial site.

The Masich tomb is fronted with the statue of a tearful dog, often decorated with a bright bow. The statue honors a pet so devoted to its master, for years it returned faithfully to the tomb. The Chapman Hyams tomb in a cemetery corner is noted for its beauty. Look inside the tiny window to see the life-size statue of an angel overcome with grief.

On the opposite side of Interstate 10, visitors will encounter a bonanza of cemeteries. Odd Fellows Rest, Greenwood Cemetery and Cypress Grove are all worth exploring, but remain cautious and alert about your surroundings.

(right) The Brunswig mausoleum is based on a tomb in Milan, Italy.

Atmosphere Abounds in Louisiana Grounds

Larry Bleiberg

New Orleans

On the outskirts of New Orleans lie two graveyards overloaded with atmosphere. One, Fleming, is bordered by a bayou and protected by a Spanish moss-trimmed live oak. The other, Holt, is New Orleans' former potter's field, where individual expression is still given free reign. Fleming is built on and around an American Indian shell mound. The plantation property was once owned by the Berthoud family, and two brothers are buried at the mound's top.

Some legends suggest that pirate Jean Lafitte is buried here, but the evidence is sketchy. The graveyard's appeal is its location—funeral processions once arrived by boat. Circling the Indian mound is a scattering of above-ground graves, some recent burials. A few tombs are graced with angels, but most are simple. It is the beautiful setting, not elaborate tombs, that catch the eye.

Fleming is reached by following State Highway 45 south of town, past the National Park Service's Barataria Preserve. Continue over a tall bridge. The road will make a hairpin turn.

Fleming Cemetery

Follow it to a stop sign, take a left and proceed 2.7 miles. The cemetery is unmarked except for a mailbox, where you will take a right on a gravel road.

At Holt, next to a police training academy, it is the tombs that demand attention. Once the burial ground for indigents who could not afford a grave, Holt is now a city-owned cemetery. Burial is inexpensive, and although there are not many elaborate gravestones here, there is plenty of imagination at work.

Some tombs could be called folk art. One burial is surrounded by what looks to be piles of junk, but it has all been carefully arranged. The snarl of broken lawn chairs, planters and carpet remnants is supposed to be a chapel adjoining a grave. Other tombs are decorated with bingo cards, beer cans and heartfelt remembrances painted on wooden tombstones. Although the grammar and spelling aren't always perfect, there is no denying the sentiment. Music fans also should take note. Buddy Bolden, who some consider the founder of jazz, is buried somewhere here in an unmarked grave.

Visitors should exercise caution in the area. Do not visit alone.

Homemade monuments grace Holt Cemetery.

Cajun Flourishes in Cemeteries, Too

Larry Bleiberg

Louisiana's French and Cajun cultures come alive in its cemeteries. Take Longfellow's poem, *Evangeline*. The fable of long-lost lovers separated during the Acadian exodus from Canada is based on a legend from St. Martinville, a picturesque south-central Louisiana town. It is under a live oak that local lore—if not Longfellow's—says Evangeline discovers that Gabriel, the man she loved, is married to another. Evangeline dies of a broken heart. It is not clear where

Emmeline Labiche, the woman said to be the inspiration for the poem, is buried. But local legend says it is next to the St. Martin de Tours Catholic Church. Visitors will find a tiny graveyard and an Evangeline statue, donated by actress Dolores del Rio, who filmed the story here in 1929. The church itself is beautiful. And take another look at that live oak. It is where governor Huey Long is said to have made his first political speech.

About twenty miles away is Lafayette, considered the capital of Cajun country. For some French flavor, visit the cemetery

at the Cathedral of St. John the Evangelist, which dates to 1822. Francophiles will find plenty of French epitaphs, from *Ici reposent*, (Here rests), to long poetic tributes carved into stone. One begins: *Quatorze ans a peine, et mourir, o mon dieu!* (Scarcely fourteen years old, and to die, oh my God!). It only gets more dramatic from there.

The cemetery also holds the bodies of two Paris-born orphan outlaws. Ernest and Alexis Blanc killed a man during a robbery in 1896. They fled to Europe, then Mexico, but returned to Louisiana when their money ran out. They were soon arrested. The brothers' confession is still studied by French students at local high schools. The men were hanged for their crime. Their graves are unmarked.

Miracles Happen, Some near Graves

Larry Bleiberg

Grand Coteau

New Orleans

For many visitors, cemeteries are places reserved for reflection and spiritual contemplation. But mention a graveyard associated with a miracle, and even non-believers pay attention. Grand Coteau, a small town north of Lafayette, is home to the only Vatican-certified miracle in North America. In 1866, a woman preparing to become a nun at the Academy of the Sacred Heart was on her deathbed. Mary Wilson's doctor had declared there was no hope, and the twenty-year-old prepared to die. The next morning, she had recovered.

Ms. Wilson died less than a year later, when she was struck by a cerebral hemorrhage. She was buried

A stylized metal branch marks Mary Wilson's simple grave.

with other sisters in a simple graveyard, beneath an iron cross. Her bedroom is now a shrine, visited by hundreds of Catholic faithful every year. The girls' school gives tours of its tranquil campus weekdays from 10 A.M. to 2 P.M. Information, (318) 662-5275.

Highlights include a small museum and copies of letters written by a Mother Superior from New York. When she heard about a Civil War battle in the vicinity of her former school, she wrote a stern letter to the Union general in charge, asking him to look out for the nuns and girls at the school. The general, who had a daughter in New York in the Mother Superior's school, did as he was told. The Academy of the Sacred Heart and its residents came to no harm.

St. Roch in New Orleans

Signs of faith also are on display at St. Roch Cemetery in New Orleans. During a yellow-fever epidemic in 1868, the parish priest made a deal with St. Roch: Protect my congregation, and we will build a shrine to you.

Apparently both parties kept to the deal.

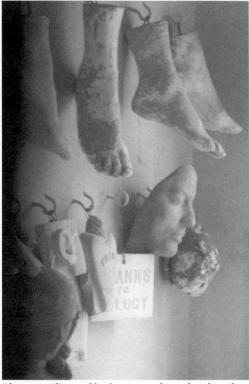

Over the years, the cemetery chapel has been visited by people who are suffering. A niche off to the side bears testimony to their recovery. Plaster feet, hearts and faces have been donated, representing past ills that have been cured. There also are braces and crutches no longer needed, and many bricks engraved with one word: "Thanks."

The chapel and cemetery are at 1725 St. Roch Ave. The chapel is open Monday through Saturday, 8:30 A.M. to 4 P.M. Do not visit alone and show caution in the neighborhood.

Plaster replicas of body parts adorn the chapel at St. Roch Cemetery.

Mississippi River Graveyards Recall Many Civil War Stories

Larry Bleiberg

St. Francisville

Baton Rouge

In a state packed with scenic cemeteries, St. Francisville just might have Louisiana's prettiest. Grace Episcopal Church has everything you could want in a graveyard: spanish moss, beautiful grounds, buildings and monuments, and a story from the Civil War. (See photo on the cover.) New Yorker John Hart was a Union officer, felled during battle. The only reason he lies with these blue-blooded families of the Old South is because he also was a Mason. As the story goes, Union and Confederate troops called a truce to bury Mr. Hart. The Mason obligation to care for fellow members was enough to stop the fighting and lay a brother to rest. Then, the battle resumed.

Other notable graveyards in the area include one in the gardens of Afton Villa, which has a tiny plantation cemetery on its grounds (admission charge). The plantation owners used the box tombs to hide silver from the Yankees. One tomb holds U.S. Senator Alexander Morris, who died in 1846. He was said to have been the most handsome man in Washington.

Across the street is Afton Villa Baptist Church, an African-American congregation, where many former slaves were buried under a moss-draped live oak. Also notable is the Rosedown Baptist Church cemetery (about a mile east of Rosedown Plantation), which

also holds former slaves. The congregation was almost kicked off its property in 1994 by the new plantation owner. The outcry from black activists, local white preservationists and the national press led to a change of heart.

Other Civil War cemeteries are found nearby.

At the Port Hudson National Cemetery are more than 250 marked graves containing some of the first black soldiers to fight—and die—for the Union. They battled at Port Hudson during a seven-week siege, believed to be the longest in U.S. military history. The black troops, members of two Louisiana regiments, joined the Union when the Confederate government refused to arm them.

Based on the soldiers' performance at Port Hudson, black troops were soon deployed elsewhere. The battlefield itself is a Louisiana state park. Although the nearby national cemetery has the familiar line of white markers, look closely at some near the entrance. The black soldiers are noted by the inscription USCT, United States Colored Troops.

To the southeast in Baton Rouge is the beautiful and historic Magnolia Cemetery. (This is not the best neighborhood, so be alert.) The burial ground is notable not only for the elaborate tombs and moss-draped oaks, but because a Civil War battle was fought here in 1862. Troops used graves and monuments for cover as they shot at one another. Bullet marks are said to be visible on some graves, although they are hard to detect more than a century later. Among the casualties were Alexander Todd, half-brother of Abraham Lincoln's wife, who fought for the Confederacy but was killed mistakenly by his own troops.

The cemetery's most notable marker has statues of three children, who died during an epidemic in 1858. After the battle, twelve Confederate soldiers were said to have been found dead behind it.

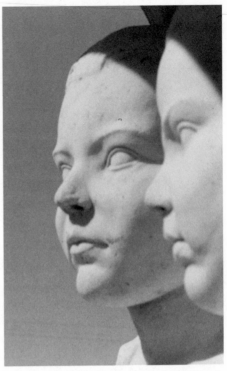

Civil War soldiers died at the foot of children's graves in Baton Rouge.

For Leprosy Patients, a Louisiana Hospital Was Home in Life and Death

Larry Bleiberg

Carville

Shunned during life, former residents of the nation's last leper colony still keep their secrets in death. Several tombs at the federal center devoted to Hansen's disease (as leprosy is now known) give only initials or nicknames. The stigma associated with the disease was so great that residents took their names to their graves.

A tour of the Gillis W. Long Hansen's Disease Center is sobering but surprisingly uplifting, too. The condition, visitors learn, can be controlled with medica-

Cemetery at the Hansen's Disease Center

tions—many developed through experiments on the armadillo, the only known animal other than humans that can harbor the disease. The story of the breakthrough was told in the 1950 bestseller, *Miracle at Carville*.

Visitors have nothing to fear. The disease is very difficult to contract, and most of the population has natural immunity. Despite popular belief, those with the ailment do not lose fingers or limbs. The disease attacks nerves and muscle control, which sometimes can disfigure limbs. The center dates to 1894 when seven lepers, as they were known then, were secreted out of New Orleans in the middle of the night on a coal barge and transported to this isolated peninsula, surrounded on three sides by the Mississippi River. Residents lived out their lives on the former sugar-cane plantation, protected from the hatred and fear of the general public. And when they died, this is where they were laid to rest.

The area was home to the family of James Carville, the colorful Democratic political consultant. He still takes an active interest in the center and was on hand to help it celebrate its 100th anniversary. But the Hansen's Center, the last facility of its type in the nation, has become a victim of its own success. Because it is unnecessary to isolate those with the disease, the center mainly serves as a research facility and provides out-patient health care. Many of the center's several hundred residents are elderly and remain not for public health reasons, but because they consider the center their home.

The government intends to shut down the institution and convert it to an alternative education center for troubled teens. The Hansen's Disease Center would move to Baton Rouge, Louisiana. Whatever its fate, there are plans to continue offering tours of the historic site. A small museum tells the center's history and remembers famous residents, such as Texan Stanley Stein (an alias for resident Sidney M. Levyson), who founded the center's magazine, circulated around the world.

Tours, available at 10 A.M. and 1 P.M., Tuesdays through Thursdays, take in the center's sprawling campus; information, (225) 642-4722. The buildings are linked with two miles of protected walkways, and bicycle is the favored mode of transportation. Many of the bikes look to be thirty or forty years old, adding to the timeless feel of the place.

And if guests ask, they also can visit the center's graveyards. The original burial ground is now a courtyard surrounded by buildings. A single marker lists those buried. The newer graveyard stands on the edge of the property. The gravestones remember those who lived out their lives here, isolated on a quiet bend of the Mississippi.

The marker listing those buried in the original burial ground

Jewish Immigrants' Final Home in Louisiana

Larry Bleiberg

Washington
Opelousas
Donaldsonville
New Orleans

Louisiana is a gumbo of cultures. Along with French, Spanish, African, Caribbean and German influences, there has long been a Jewish presence in this region. Note the Hebrew epitaphs found in Jewish cemeteries throughout the state. And on gravestones carved in English, you will see birthplaces in France, Germany, Poland and other European locales.

Jews immigrated to Louisiana during the eighteenth and nineteenth centuries and, as with other ethnic groups, began burial societies. In many small towns, the Jewish community has disappeared—many moved to larger cities or west into Texas. It is only in cemeteries that these residents are remembered.

Bikur Shalom cemetery in Donaldsonville—between New Orleans and Baton Rouge—is a small plot, but it provides an introduction to Jewish burial practices. For most Jews in Louisiana, the custom is to bury in the soil, so there are not mausoleums. The practice comes from the phrase in Genesis: "From dust you are, and to dust you shall return." In keeping with tradition, some graves use copings, above-ground frames filled with dirt.

A few tombs have small stones placed on top, a sign someone has recently visited. The practice, which honors the dead, began centuries ago when graves were marked with rock mounds. Those who left a stone helped maintain it. Otherwise, the Jewish cemeteries are similar to their fellow Louisiana graveyards: Some have elaborate tombs, wild stories and heartfelt grave makers.

Take the Donaldsonville tomb of a nine-year-old boy named Morris. He died in 1920 and a black-and-white photograph embedded in the gravestone shows the lost son as he once looked. It is topped with a stone dove. Sitting by itself in the far corner of the cemetery is the tomb of a Jewish man said to have been a vagabond. When he fell ill, no rabbi could be found, so he received his last rites from a priest.

Near Lafayette are small cemeteries in the cities of Opelousas and Washington. Recently, the only sign of life at Washington's Hebrew Rest cemetery was an animal trap placed atop a grave. Buried here are members of the Wolff family, who were former city mayors and bank presidents.

By contrast, New Orleans' Jewish cemeteries are still used. One of the oldest, Hebrew Rest has a nice collection of angels, statues and Hebrew inscriptions. The human figures indicate the cemetery holds Reform Jews not Orthodox, who generally do not erect elaborate monuments. The well-kept cemetery dates to 1860, and was expanded in 1894. It is surrounded by an ornate iron fence, and is built on a natural ridge that allowed for in-ground burial. Most graves face the east, toward the rising sun and Jerusalem.

Paying Tribute to the Blues

Kathryn Straach

Mooringsport

Wortham

Two graves in unassuming cemeteries outside one-light towns are the final resting places of a couple of the greatest blues artists of all time: "Blind" Lemon Jefferson in Wortham, Texas, and Huddie "Leadbelly" Ledbetter in Mooringsport, Louisiana. For a short time in the early part of this century, their careers overlapped, and the duo traveled together through Houston, Dallas, Shreveport and all points in between. The original blues brothers, you might say.

Blind Lemon

In 1928, Blind Lemon sang "See That My Grave Is Kept Clean," and it appears he's getting his wish. Blind Lemon's tidy grave is in the African-American section of the Wortham cemetery, a few miles from where he was born in Couchman, and about twenty miles south of Corsicana. Not much is known about his childhood other than he was born blind and he played in the streets of Wortham for nickels and dimes.

And not much is known about his death in 1929. Stories range from foul play, to passing out in a snowbank, to getting left in a street after a fight. What is known: He was a blues great. He recorded eighty-nine songs in just under four years, and he is believed to have influenced just about every blues singer who followed him, including Louis Armstrong.

To view his grave, take Interstate 45 south to Richland; exit on State Highway 14. Go south 10 miles. When you reach the Wortham Cemetery sign, you've gone just a little too far. The entrance to the separate cemetery is through a metal gate just before. It looks as if you are entering someone's ranch, complete with cattle guard.

Blind Lemon's grave is easy to spot back along the chain-link fence because the marble headstone, with "Lemon Jefferson" in large letters, is new. It was placed there in 1997 by a group of blues musicians. In front is a bronze plaque placed by the Texas Historical Society in 1967.

Guitar picks, as well as nickels and dimes, can be seen in a concrete cup in front of the marker.

Leadbelly

No one can accuse Huddie Ledbetter of being a saint, but he had a way with music. While serving a thirty-year prison term in Huntsville for killing a man, he composed and sang a tune to the governor, successfully pleading for his release. (He served more time later for other offenses.) "Goodnight Irene" and "Midnight Special" are just a couple of the hundreds of songs—mostly popular with white audiences—he produced during his heyday.

In 1949, Leadbelly traveled overseas, hoping to build a European audience, but he began suffering from muscle spasms. He was diagnosed with Lou Gehrig's disease and died by the end of the year. To visit his grave, just across the line in Louisiana, take State Highway 169 north from Interstate 20 for about 8 miles. Six miles before you get to Mooringsport (there's a sign), turn left at the light. Drive 2 miles; on your left is Shiloh Baptist Church. The cemetery is directly behind.

You immediately know which grave is Leadbelly's—it's the only one with a black wrought-iron fence around it. The recent marker is a tall black stone listing his many accomplishments:

> Huddie (Lead Belly) Ledbetter, 1889–1949. A Louisiana Legend Has Been Duly Elected to: The Songwriters Hall of Fame, New York, 1972; The Nashville Songwriters Hall of Fame, Nashville, TN, 1980; The Rock and Roll Hall of Fame, New York, 1988; The Southern Songwriters Hall of Fame, Shreveport, LA, 1989; Northwest Louisiana Hall of Fame, Bossier City, LA, 1991.

A large black granite marker on the ground is etched with a gray guitar and reads, "King of the 12 String Guitar." Coins have been tossed on top. Several other Ledbetters are buried nearby. If it were not for his grave, the small rural cemetery would look almost forgotten. Many of the graves have no tombstones. Artificial flowers have faded. A basketball goal on the other side of the fence has a distinctive lean.

See also p. 196 for a listing of National Cemeteries in Louisiana.

More on Cemeteries

National Cemeteries Are Local Gems

Bob Bersano

Texas and its neighbors support fourteen national cemeteries. Each is a national shrine but also a community project. And each depends on local citizenry to maintain and operate the site. Volunteers prepare burial grounds for ceremonies on Memorial and Veterans days. Veterans groups assist by indexing grave locations, planting flowers or guiding visitors. Scouts decorate graves. Rifle and honor squads provide military honors at burials. Citizenry donate trees, benches and monuments.

Following is a listing of regional national cemeteries. Call for specific hours of operations, events and ceremonies, and other information.

Texas

- **Fort Bliss National Cemetery**, 5200 Fred Wilson Road, El Paso 79906; (915) 564-0201.
- **Fort Sam Houston National Cemetery**, 1520 Harry Wurzbach Road, San Antonio 78209; (210) 820-3891.
- **San Antonio National Cemetery**, 517 Paso Hondo St., San Antonio 78202; (210) 820-3891.
- **Houston National Cemetery**, 104110 Veterans Memorial Drive, Houston 77038; (281) 447-8686.
- **Kerrville National Cemetery**, VA Medical Center, 3600 Memorial Blvd., Kerrville 78028; (210) 820-3891.

New Mexico

- **Fort Bayard National Cemetery**, P.O. Box 189, Fort Bayard 88036; (915) 564-0201.
- **Santa Fe National Cemetery**, 501 N. Guadalupe St., Santa Fe 87501; (505) 988-6400.

Oklahoma

- **Fort Gibson National Cemetery**, Rt. 2, Box 47, 1423 Cemetery Road, Fort Gibson 74434; (918) 478-2334.

Arkansas

- **Fayetteville National Cemetery**, 700 Government Ave., Fayetteville 72701; (501) 444-5051.
- **Fort Smith National Cemetery**, 522 Garland Ave., Fort Smith 72901; (501) 783-5345.
- **Little Rock National Cemetery**, 2523 Confederate Blvd., Little Rock 72206; (501) 324-6401.

Louisiana

- **Alexandria National Cemetery**, 209 E. Shamrock Ave., Pineville 71360; (601) 445-4981.
- **Baton Rouge National Cemetery**, 220 N. 19th St., Baton Rouge 70806; (504) 654-3767.
- **Port Hudson National Cemetery**, 20978 Port Hickey Road, Zachary 70791; (504) 654-3767.

Grave Blooms Preserve a Bit of History

Bob Bersano

Their faces brighten hallowed grounds and pay tribute to the deceased—enduring rain, drought, icy weather or anything else that Mother Nature sends their way. Their numbers multiply over time, but despite their abundance, they often go unnoticed when others seek out friends and relatives. They are the guardians of the past, present and future, asking for nothing in return.

They are the old cemetery flowers. The ones that flourish without any watering, fertilizing, dividing or pruning. They're at home where they are and don't require anything from anyone. The irises, roses, day lilies, daffodils, oleanders, cedar shrubs and roses, many planted by Texas settlers in honor of their deceased kin. Field Roebuck of Dallas knows many of these old cemeteries well. Whenever he's on the road for business or pleasure, Mr. Roebuck, a consulting engineer, geologist and plant fancier, builds time into his schedule to go exploring for some of the state's earliest settlers and their most prized possessions—the beloved plants they brought to Texas. And, occasionally, when he sees a beautiful flower, especially an old rose, he'll take a cutting and try to get it to grow in his yard. It can be difficult to identify these old-timers, though. It was easier for Mr. Roebuck to find the burial place of his father's brother, who died at age two early in the century, than it has been to identify the beautiful, nearly 100-year-old "smelly" rose shrub he discovered thriving near the infant's stone.

"I was at a reunion when the subject of my uncle came up from a couple of genealogists in my family," says Mr. Roebuck. "I knew where he was supposed to be buried" (in Sardis Cemetery on State Highway 1512 outside Jewett, Texas).

"I found my uncle's stone easily, but then I spotted an old red climbing rose that had spread out nearly twenty feet. I call the rose a 'mothproof mauve' because even the foliage has an odor of cedar."

He has been unsuccessful at formally identifying the plant. He hopes to bring a bloom from the rose to a Historical Rose Society gathering soon in the hope someone attending the event might know.

Discovering old plants "is kind of like finding an arrowhead or a fossil. I enjoy the detective work involved in identifying these old plants," Mr. Roebuck says.

He's not alone.

Many people share Mr. Roebuck's love for old flowers, shrubs and trees, and they've formed groups such as the Texas Rose Rustlers (713) 453-1274 and the Dallas Area Historical Rose Society (DAHRS), P. O. Box 831448, Richardson, TX 75083-1448; web site: *http//community. dallasnews.com/dmn/theyellowrose*. While these groups don't limit themselves to cemeteries, they do rate them high on their lists of plant sources.

For those who might enjoy discovering old cemeteries for themselves, Mr. Roebuck recommends carrying a copy of the *The Roads of Texas* atlas (Shearer Publishing, $14.95) in their vehicles when they travel. It leads the way to hundreds of cemeteries throughout the state. Shearer also published *Roads of Louisiana*, *Roads of Arkansas*, *Roads of Oklahoma*, and *Roads of New Mexico*. The avid plant man never leaves home without his Texas atlas. His latest find? The Perryman Cemetery in Montague County outside Forestburg, Texas. He has found two more as-yet-unidentified roses flourishing there. But sooner or later he'll find their names.

Do no harm

The key to taking cuttings from old cemeteries is to show respect for both the place and the plant, says Mr. Roebuck.

"Don't do anything that would harm the plant," he says.

Mike Shoup couldn't agree more. If it weren't for the old plants Mr.

Shoup discovered in Texas cemeteries and elsewhere, his Antique Rose Emporium in Brenham, Texas, might have been more difficult to establish. It sells an array of native plants, including old roses, irises and day lilies. Many of his roses were first planted in the mid-1800s, plants that Texas settlers brought with them.

"Cemeteries have been a fantastic source of plants for me and my business," Mr. Shoup says. "Those old cemetery flowers and plants are the best ones to grow in Texas yards because they're survivors. They simply don't require much care."

Though the public is welcome at most cemeteries, Mr. Shoup strongly recommends following protocol.

"Most old cemeteries don't have caretakers, so your own ethical standards should guide you in unlabeled cemeteries." If there is a cemetery office, always go there first and tell them what you'd like to do, then respect their wishes. "Never ever dig a plant up; cuttings will do just fine."

Think of cemetery plants as little bits of history, Mr. Shoup suggests. "Growing the plants at your home helps preserve their heritage."

Index